Dr. Karl Albrecht is a management consultant, seminar leader, professional speaker, and a prolific writer. He works with business executives to increase organizational effectiveness through management teamwork, effective problem solving, and innovation. His book *Brainpower: Learn to Improve Your Thinking Skills,* available from Prentice Hall Press, was the basis for the best-selling training film of the same name, starring John Houseman.

Books by Karl Albrecht, Ph.D.

Successful Management by Objectives: An Action Manual   1978

Stress and the Manager: Making It Work for You   1979

Brain Power: Learn to Improve Your Thinking Skills 1980

Organization Development: A Total Systems Approach to Positive Change in Any Business Organization   1983

Brain Building: Easy Games to Develop Your Problem Solving Skills   1983

Idea Power: How To Get Ahead by Getting Smarter 1985

KARL ALBRECHT, Ph.D

Successful Management by Objectives

An Action Manual

PRENTICE
HALL
PRESS

New York   London   Toronto   Sydney   Tokyo   Singapore

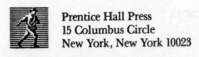

Prentice Hall Press
15 Columbus Circle
New York, New York 10023

Published in 1988 by Prentice Hall Press
Originally published by Prentice-Hall, Inc.

Library of Congress Cataloging-in-Publication Data

ALBRECHT, KARL G
  Successful management by objectives.

Includes bibliographical references and index.
  1. Management by objectives.   I. Title.
HD31.A356   658.4   77-14971
ISBN 0-13-863258-8

Manufactured in the United States of America

25 24 23 22 21 20

Contents

v

Preface

"You've just told me there's no Santa Claus," mourned one manager during a recent seminar on management by objectives. We had just finished reviewing contemporary approaches to "MBO," and she had begun to realize how often the popular "install-an-MBO-system" approach has failed to deliver the expected results. In fact, about one-fifth of the participants in that workshop mentioned having been closely associated with one or more MBO programs which they considered unsuccessful, or even outright failures.

For over ten years, the customary approach to management by objectives has operated as if there were some kind of a *system* — almost like a physical apparatus — which a manager could buy from a consultant, or could design and install after reading the right book. The manager, in this view, could simply bring in the system, plug it in like an air conditioner or some other piece of hardware, and automatically enjoy the benefits of better living through modern management.

But an alarming number of MBO failures has resulted from mistaking an overdesigned administrative framework for the basic process of objectives-oriented managing. Many MBO specialists have installed system after system, only to watch them collapse under their own weight, or be sabotaged by the membership at large of the client organization. One university professor lamented that "Of *Fortune* magazine's 500 top corporations, only half indicated they had active MBO programs any-where in their organizations. Of those, only 20 per cent actually had effective programs. I would have expected more." Clearly, we need a reliable way to make management by objectives *work.* Most of these "programs" haven't done the job.

Practicing managers are growing increasingly disenchanted with the standard mechanistic approach, and with the sometimes naive management literature which prescribes it. When practical experience diverges so widely from theory, then theory has got to give. We need, and we are now developing, a "system-less" approach to management by objectives which avoids the *"Rigor-Mortis* Trap," the "Paper Mill," and the attendant Rat Race.

I believe management by objectives as a discipline will now enter a new and creative phase in which the focus will be on *people,* not on systems. If we can develop a fundamental approach to organizational life which promotes payoff-oriented thinking, rewarding human environments in our organizations and honest respect for the needs and potentials of American workers, then we will be free to *use* our systems and methods, rather than be used by them.

In this book, I've tried to focus on the basic *concept* of management by objectives, as well as the fundamental principles of human behavior which support it. I've tried to make the book a complete and self-contained treatment of the subject. The reader who is looking for another cookbook on "how to install an MBO system" will not find it here. How-ever, the reader who wants to know how to *manage* by objectives will indeed find a thorough treatment of that subject.

This book defines management by objectives as a *managerial behavior pattern,* not a formal paper system. From this definition, we can specify the effective behaviors required of managers and workers, and we can define the "ecological" aspects of the human organization which form the foundation for growth and performance.

It will probably take us another ten or fifteen years to completely bury the mechanistic tradition, and to establish effective managerial *behavior* as the foundation of management by objectives. This book is an attempt to help that constructive revolution along its way.

KARL ALBRECHT. Ph.d
San Diego, California

1

Basic Principles of
Management by Objectives

The Problem of
Organizational Effectiveness

For as long as mankind has had formal organizations, those who have directed and controlled them have found themselves faced with the same question: "How well are we doing what we are doing?" The notion of an organization as an abstract entity—as a *system*—is not new. Nor is the concept of professional management; its origins are lost in history. We may choose to believe that twentieth-century society has spawned the management profession, that its tools and techniques are distinctly modern. This is not so. Management may be the world's oldest profession.

As long ago as 4000 B.C. the Egyptians and Sumerians developed systems of planning and record keeping. The Egyptians are credited with recognizing the need for planning, organizing, and controlling the activities of large groups of workers. The concept of decentralized organization is at least 2000 years old. Hammurabi established a minimum-wage system as early as 1800 B.C. The Chinese developed planning and control systems as early as 1100 B.C. In 400 B.C., Socrates enunciated the universality of the management function in organized human endeavor. In

1

350 B.C., Plato espoused the principle of specialization for human efficiency. Alexander the Great made brilliant use of the military-staff system in 325 B.C. In 1436, the famous Arsenal of Venice employed over 1000 people in shipbuilding and armament, making extensive use of accounting systems, planning, inventory control, assembly-line techniques, interchangeable parts, and a formal system of personnel management. In 1881, Joseph Wharton established college courses in business management at the University of Pennsylvania.[1]

In all of these endeavors, the problem of how to make organizations function more effectively has been the central theme of analysis, experimentation, and design. Why one army defeats another; why one country grows and flourishes while another declines and decays; why one corporation grows and profits handsomely while another languishes; why one small business enterprise after another goes bankrupt; why a government agency is abolished; why one nonprofit institution flounders and dies while another exerts a dynamic force for social improvement—these are questions of performance.

Organizational effectiveness is also defined situationally, of course. The right timing, the right national mood, the "hot" new product, the untapped demand for a social service, the charisma of its leaders, the special skills and political acumen of its top executive, lucky events in its environment—all play a part in the health and development of any enterprise. But through all the ups and downs, through all the lucky and unlucky changes in the environment, with all the lucky and unlucky guesses about what to do, one variable stands out as most instrumental in organizational effectiveness. That variable is *managerial performance*—the ability of a small group of key individuals to chart a course and to guide the efforts of others along it. Managerial performance always forms a key element of an organization's effectiveness.

The Search for Better
Management Technique

Most organizations are reasonably well managed. Despite the complaints of many workers, despite the ups and downs of virtually all

---

[1]Claude S. George, Jr., *The History of Management Thought* (Englewood Cliffs, NJ: Prentice-Hall, Inc.,) 1965, pp. xiii-xvii.

corporate enterprise, despite the accusations of waste and inefficiency levelled at military and government agencies, most organizations manage to combine the efforts of diverse individuals quite constructively. Some organizations are more effective than others, but comparatively few meet with disaster.

Most managers settle for "reasonably" good performance. Of the more than eight million managers in America, perhaps seven million of them get along on a "reasonable" complement of cognitive and social skills and adapt "reasonably" well to the changes and problems which confront them. They manage "reasonably" effective organizations.

Throughout the centuries, however, a small minority of managers has been unwilling to settle for reasonably effective organizational performance. They have been impatient with reasonable results, unsatisfied with merely reasonable personal skills. They have sought managerial excellence. They have sought to understand the dynamics of organizations, the problems of coping with a changing environment, the behavior patterns of people at work, the complex social processes within human systems, the methods of analysis and design, and—above all—themselves as managers. Those who have experimented with new methods and concepts have pointed the way to others. They have shown how to apply their techniques to organizational management and have demonstrated them in action. But excellence is not for everyone. By the very definition of the word, it implies that only a small number of managers will experiment; will try new ideas; will change and grow; and that the great majority will settle for reasonable performance.

However, what was excellence yesterday is now an accepted standard of performance. At the turn of the century, Frederick Taylor's methods of "scientific management" were new, bold, and unproven.[2] Today, the entire science of industrial engineering revolves around Taylor's basic principles. And, similarly, what is excellence today in management will gradually be learned and applied by the many and will become the basis for reasonable managerial effectiveness in five, ten, and twenty years.

The topic of this book is managerial excellence.

[2]Frederick W. Taylor, *Principles of Scientific Management* (New York: Harper & Bros., 1913).

Basic Facts about
Managerial Performance

Behavioral scientists have had an extended field day—forty years, at least—studying managerial "effectiveness." Research projects, statistical analyses, psychological tests, theories of leadership, and training theories have piled up higher than those who have developed them. For all the frustrating attempts of behavioral researchers to analyze and classify the elements of the manager's performance, precious little is known which was not already derived generations ago by commonsense thinking. Here are some of the major findings of commonsense.

First, those who manage well seem to be acutely aware of themselves as managers. They see themselves as executing a special social function, quite apart from providing particular knowledge and expertise in the areas of their organizational operation. Everyday experience in the business world gives us many examples of highly qualified and talented technical experts who fail miserably as managers for lack of basic social skills or of the practical skills of planning and organizing the work which needs to be done. People often describe this person as "a fish out of water"—meaning, of course, that he is relatively oblivious to the more abstract portion of his job which requires skills and actions entirely separate from his primary form of expertise. The high-performance manager tends to be a highly self-aware person.

Second, those who manage well tend to study management as a practice. They read about management. They discuss management techniques with their colleagues. They consider problems from the special vantage point of their positions as managers. Whereas the reasonably skilled manager tends to see himself as the chief protagonist in a problem-solving situation, personally facing the challenges presented by the environment, the high-performance manager tends to see himself as a mobilizer. This person thinks in terms of cleverly bringing human resources to bear upon a problem, and of getting the problem solved by magnifying the consequences of what he does. In this respect, the case of the "manager" who refuses to delegate is a commonplace occurrence in business. The harried, overstressed "workaholic" manager is preoccupied with solving problems rather than with getting them solved. The high-performance manager mobilizes human resources.

Third, those who manage well tend to study themselves and their interactions with others. They see the management skill as an extremely comprehensive one, spanning an enormous range of conceptual, technical, and human problems and situations. They are often committed to self-development as an avenue to managerial excellence. They are not content with the *status quo*. They do not find much satisfaction in simply struggling through another harrowing day. Rather, they pride themselves in managing well. They read, they study, they discuss ideas, they take an active interest in life itself. They are committed to their own personal growth, for their own personal reasons, and the organizations they manage usually benefit from the effects of their growth.

Fourth, those who manage well seem to take every possible opportunity to "get ahead" of their problems—to gain the initiative on the environment in such a way that events tend to unfold as they would like them to, or at least as they have anticipated. The classic "muddle-through" manager, as described by Charles E. Lindblom,[3] tends to act only when forced to. This person acts as a relatively passive functionary with no clear purpose other than to prevent or control disruptions in the day-to-day routine of business. The muddle-through manager makes decisions based on the obiously available alternatives, and generally chooses those courses of action which minimize change to the organization. On the other hand, Peter Drucker's "entrepreneurial" manager[4] tends to accept change as a part of the business of managing. This manager makes use of opportunities, and accepts risk as an element of the problem-solving and goal-setting process. The manager who manages reasonably well may be described as a *reactive manager*. The high-performance manager might be described as an *assertive manager*.

This fourth element, the assertive attitude, forms a key aspect of managing by objectives. The entrepreneurial manager, to whom the forward-looking, assertive attitude comes easily, focuses on objectives as a natural way of doing business. For the reactive, muddle-through manager, it may be an unfathomable mystery, or a way to devise a new gimmick for keeping his organization under control, or possibly a way to develop into an assertive, high-performance manager.

These features of high-performance management and "reasonably"

[3]Charles Lindblom, *The Intelligence of Democracy* (New York: The Free Press, 1965).
[4]Peter F. Drucker, *The Effective Executive* (New York: Harper & Row, 1967).

good management imply a comprehensive definition of the high-performance manager. This person has at least four major dimensions to his functioning, namely:

1. Strategist — One who looks to the future, makes educated guesses about the major forces and trends he can see, and interprets them in terms of opportunities for growth and progress
2. Problem solver — One who clearly perceives the differences between the anticipated future and the unfolding present, and who decides what must be done with those factors under his control to influence the environment or to adapt to it most effectively
3. Leader — One who offers those who answer to him a clear course of action which will gain their commitment and serve their individual objectives as well as the higher objectives of the organization
4. Teacher — One who guides others, helps them to identify and solve problems, to work effectively at what they do, and to develop themselves as individuals as well as workers

In all of these functions, the manager operates to shape human activity. By giving directions, the manager intervenes constructively in the multitude of work activities going on about him, and gives them a common meaning. Only the manager can bring together the efforts of many people and focus them on the accomplishment of worthwhile goals.

Basic Facts of Organizational Life

Let's keep our study of management by objectives focused on the realities of the workworld as we know them. In order to make sense out of the basic principles, we will need models of everyday organizational life and of normal human behavior which correspond to our actual experiences. Many of the pitfalls of conventional management theories stem from abstract, unreal models of organizations which could never really exist. They leave out much of the human side — the everyday, commonplace, and significant activities which go on in every single human organization we know about. In this discussion, let's put back these significant human elements and deal with them just as forthrightly as we deal with the more abstract aspects of organizations.

First, let us note that not everyone in an organization can be "happy," or contented, or fulfilled at all times. It would be unrealistic to expect that. At any one time, some of the members—including managers—will be operating in a highly rewarding mode. They will be doing work which they consider worthwhile and which they enjoy. They will feel involved and highly committed to their roles in the organization. Others will feel alienated, frustrated, and dissatisfied. They will be operating in nonrewarding modes, perhaps accomplishing little, and getting little satisfaction from their transactions with the organization. Some of them may be considering departure from the unit, some may be trying to change their conditions, and others may be suffering passively in silence. And a very large category of people within the organization will probably be "doing all right." They will be handling their jobs reasonably well, accomplishing a reasonable amount, and gaining reasonable psychic and material rewards for what they do.

A practical view of the manager's role in creating a healthy organizational climate calls for maximizing the number of people who are operating in a committed and reward-getting mode. But we must acknowledge that, as a practical matter, we will always find a certain fraction of the members alienated and operating unproductively. The manager needs to think in terms of minimizing this number in every way practically possible, but need not go to idealistic extremes. Just as the American work force displays a statistical residue of unemployed people despite the health of the nation's economy, any organization will have a momentary "noise level" of alienation and discontent. Trying to please everyone will surely lead to pleasing no one.

Obviously, high-performance management will minimize the number of alienated and unproductive people in the organization at any one time. A mass walkout in a nonunion plant would, for example, constitute a clear signal that alienation has become a significant management problem, not merely a statistical minimum. This practical view of employee attitude offers an avenue for assessing the health and strength of the overall organization, since employee attitude is linked very closely to productivity.

The objectives-oriented manager, realizing that employee commitment to the organization's goals is all important to success, tries to sense and evaluate the attitudes of the members of the organization frequently and realistically. This practical-minded manager realizes that a certain level of griping and complaining is not pathological or harmful, but represents a normal outlet for the everyday stresses of work life. But he also realizes that widespread complaining, especially about the same topic, signals an underlying condition which could adversely affect organizational performance. The alert manager is thick-skinned enough to overlook the everyday noise level of complaints, but sensitive enough to detect the signals of impending dissatisfaction and alienation which may portend organizational crisis.

A basic fact of life in many organizations is employee cynicism. In some organizations, especially large ones, the employees have been alienated so thoroughly, and for so long, that virtually any change made by the organization's managers—no matter how well intentioned— is greeted with suspicion, cynical criticism, and perhaps even the active intention to subvert it. In such a case, managers must deal with the cynical reactions in order to bring about constructive change.

These factors point up sharply the effects of organizational climate on the success of management ventures. Employee attitude is not simply a trivial side effect; it is a basic element of managerial success. It is both a *cause* of success (or failure) and a *symptom* of it.

A certain amount of confusion also characterizes everyday organizational life. Communication breakdowns, misunderstandings, and human mistakes play a regular part in getting work done. They may range from the trivial or even amusing to the serious or even pathological. Just as with employee satisfaction, the manager can sense and evaluate this variable as a means of determining how well the organization is operating. The objectives-oriented manager realizes that a certain amount of confusion and misalignment of resources is inevitable in any human system, but also realizes that an unusual amount of confusion and misalignment signals an organization which has lost its sense of direction. The assertive manager relies on clearly understood objectives as measures of organizational accomplishment and realizes that much of the effort in a human system tends to be *self-aligning* if its members understand the unit's goals and commit themselves to their achievement.

The objectives-oriented manager also takes a practical view of human politics as a fact of organizational life. People often compete with one another for power and status, and they maintain personal alliances and "treaties" which enable them to wield influence within the human system. The enlightened manager realizes that every organization has a grapevine which carries important news far and wide throughout the system. He acknowledges these facts as important and as potentially healthy for the organization. The objectives-oriented manager realizes that, by providing the organization's members with a common set of goals and by giving meaning to their accomplishments, he can shape these human energies to useful ends. He does not fret about the waste of a small amount of energy caused by rivalry and personal self-interest. But he does continually sense and evaluate the social processes within the organization, staying alert for major developments which might undermine the concentration of the members' energies toward worthwhile accomplishments.

In trying to foster a sense of identification and commitment on the part of the employees, the manager comes face-to-face with another fact of organizational life—a particularly cruel one. This is the fact that virtually every member of a typical organization perceives and reacts to the *formal division of roles* between "managers" and "workers" — between the controllers and the controlled. The most idealistic form of participative management must sooner or later recognize that the majority of the organization's members see themselves as formally taking direction from a select group. The manager belongs to this ingroup, and very little he can do short of abdicating his responsibilities can change this perception.

In fact, very few of the members of a typical business organization would advocate changing this feature of organizational life—save, perhaps, for replacing a few selected managers. This relationship between managers and employees is such a fundamental fact of life that many managers completely overlook its influence on employee attitudes. But employees seldom overlook it. Communication between these two role-locked individuals reflects their individual perspectives on the relationship.

The manager may assume that an employee will tell him anything of significance which he as a manager needs to know. He may anticipate and feel entitled to honesty and candor from the employee. He may feel that his constructive attitude and honest intentions justify a childlike openness and transparency on the part of the employee.

The employee, on the other hand, is generally acutely aware of the manager's role as potential punisher and less aware of his role as a potential rewarder. He learns, over the course of his relationship with the manager, what subjects are "safe" to discuss, and what things are safe to say about them. The employee quite properly approaches the communication transaction with his own best interests in mind. The employee usually wants to do a good job, to keep management informed, and to deal with day-to-day problems frankly and openly, *after* assuring himself that he will not jeopardize his own needs and goals by doing so. In the best of situations, the manager must communicate with employees who continually check and double-check to see their own interests are well-served in the transaction. Indeed, the manager communicates with his own boss in the same way. In the worst of situations, the manager may deal with an employee who is alienated, frustrated, cynical, or uncooperative.

Because management by objectives depends for its success on the extent of employee involvement and commitment to the organization's purposes, the manager must use a great deal of skill in day-to-day communication processes and must establish a climate in which the perceived differences between managers and employees operate to focus human energy rather than to dissipate it.

Activity: The Stuff of Which Organizational Life Is Made

If we could make ourselves invisible and go into a typical organization to observe its processes, and if we could somehow see everyone in the organization simultaneously—take a snapshot at an instant in time—we would observe eight different kinds of human activity. They are:

1. Production—Activity which directly produces the products or provides the services which are the basic mission of the organization
2. Production Support—Activity which directly supports the Production Activities
3. Organizational Maintenance—Activities which makes the organization work, e.g., sales, record keeping, analysis, design, personnel, public relations, plant security, etc.
4. Management—Activity which establishes and maintains the basic course of the organization and ensures its continued existence
5. Busy Work—Activity assigned to people by managers purely for show, i.e., to give the appearance of accomplishment
6. Make-Believe Work—Activity of those who are trying to give the appearance of constructive accomplishment

7. Personal Activities—Activities which serve the private interests of individuals, e.g., telephoning a friend, tending to a family matter, eating a snack, photocopyng a recipe, pilfering paper clips, or revising one's resume

8. Social Activities—Activities which service interpersonal relationships, e.g., grapevine gossip, stopping to chat with a co-worker, drinking coffee together, or passing out union literature

Most of conventional management theory completely ignores the last four kinds of activity on this list. Yet these activities go on in every single human organization on the face of the earth. Indeed, the last two are required for organizational health. Any useful theory of management will have to account for these "nontheoretical" forms of human activity, and will have to deal with them as part of the reality of managing.

A common implication in many theories or systems for management is that the manager's task is to ruthlessly eliminate the four "unproductive" activities of Busy Work, Make-Believe Work, Personal Activities, and Social Activities. Not only is this notion theoretically shaky, but as a practical matter it is simply impossible. A more enlightened view holds that the manager should influence others in such a way as to achieve an *effective balance* among all eight of the functional-activity categories.

Assuming for the moment that the first four categories of activity are self-evidently required for organizational effectiveness, let's examine the other four more carefully. The following views are rather heretical compared to current literature dealing with management by objectives.

Let's consider the category of Personal Activities. Is there a manager anywhere in an American business institution who never makes a personal telephone call, never takes a few minutes off to discuss his child's problems with the high school counsellor; never takes an extended lunch break to tend to some errands; never browses through the morning paper over coffee during the first few minutes of the day; never takes a few minutes to clip a cartoon out of a magazine and hang it up on the wall beside his desk? Any manager could easily justify these activities on his own part. Yet many managers seem to feel that it is wrong for employees (who, after all, *are* a different species) to spend any time at all on Personal Activities.

What about Social Activities? Is there a manager who never stops to chat with a friend in the hallway; who never tarries over lunch, enjoying a friendly conversation; who never flirts with a member of the opposite sex; or, indeed, who never spends time making friends with other managers who are important to career success? Should the manager's attitudes toward employee behavior be any different? To what extent should we disapprove of Busy-Work types of activities? Theoretically, one hundred percent. No one *should* be assigned by a manager to do things which have no real organizational value; which merely delude the onlooker into believing that constructive work is underway. Yet as a practical matter we know that in every organization, at least a small portion of time is wasted in Busy Work.

Similarly, at least a small portion of the energy in every organization goes into Make-Believe Work. Every manager, at some moment or other, feels less than one hundred percent enthusiastic about the huge pile of work facing him. The manager may feel restless, a bit bored, or even a bit resentful at having so much work to do. Such a person's natural inclination may be to go for a walk, or put his feet up and daydream, or to take a catnap. But if the manager believes these excapist activities would be noticed and condemned by others whose good will he values, he will probably not induldge in them directly. This person will probably meet his needs, which are quite normal and human, by some form of activity which gives the proper "appearance," and which allows him to relax and refresh his mind. The honest forms of activity which would serve these needs are commonly referred to by the universally known term: "goofing off." In most American organizations, managers are not at liberty to goof off. Nor are workers. Both managers and workers often meet their personal needs for mental refreshment surreptitiously, by Make-Believe Work. Lest the reader conclude that I advocate a "country-club" approach to organizational management, I will state a basic thesis which is the foundation of an effective approach to management by objectives. That thesis is this: *the manager's job is not to tell people how to act; it is to show them what has to be accomplished, and to help them accomplish it.* Activity should follow from goal setting. We need not condone wasteful or unproductive forms of activity, but we cannot really stamp them out by direct attack. The manager must lead the employees to substitute more effective forms of behavior for the old forms.

The members of every organization need a sense of "pace." They need the impetus which a strong leader provides to keep their attention focussed on meaningful activity leading to worthwhile results. Indeed, one of the constant challenges facing any leader is to establish a "proper" pace for the individuals under his influence. The manager must prompt them in a general way to work hard and well. He must demand and expect performance. And he must respect their human capacities for fatigue, keeping the work pressures within bounds which are reasonable over the long run.

Any reasonably aware visitor to an ongoing work situation can easily sense the pace—the intensity level of the activity going on there. The pace within an organizational unit can vary from lackadaisical to frenetic. Most human beings can adapt to extreme variations in the pace of work, but they tend to be acutely aware of the long-term "average" pace. As Figure 1-1 shows, the attitudes of members of an organizational unit reflect fairly directly the average intensity level to which they are subjected. At one extreme, the "country-club" atmosphere, one finds detachment and boredom. At the other extreme, the "sweat shop," one finds frustration, resentment, and even hostility. Both of these extremes limit organizational performance and threaten the emotional well-being of the people themselves.

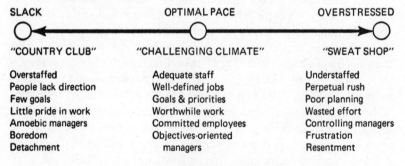

SLACK	OPTIMAL PACE	OVERSTRESSED
"COUNTRY CLUB"	"CHALLENGING CLIMATE"	"SWEAT SHOP"
Overstaffed	Adequate staff	Understaffed
People lack direction	Well-defined jobs	Perpetual rush
Few goals	Goals & priorities	Poor planning
Little pride in work	Worthwhile work	Wasted effort
Amoebic managers	Committed employees	Controlling managers
Boredom	Objectives-oriented	Frustration
Detachment	managers	Resentment

Figure 1-1
Each Organization Has a Characteristic "Pace" of Activity

The Activity Trap

C. Northcote Parkinson enunciated a cynical but true principle of human activity in his famous Parkinson's Law: "The Work (i.e., activity) Expands to Fill up the Time Available for Its Completion."[5]

[5]C. Northcote Parkinson, *Parkinson's Law* (New York: Houghton & Mifflin Company, 1964), p. 15.

This is a fact of life in a great many organizations, and it stems directly from the influence—or lack of it—of the organization's leaders in showing the people what must be accomplished. A classic story, told many times to illustrate people's perceptions of what they do, goes as follows:

An elderly gentleman, strolling along a country road in England many years ago, stopped to watch a group of stone cutters who were apparently beginning a construction project. He approached one of the men and inquired off-handledly, "What are you doing?" "I'm working," muttered the man, and said nothing more. The old gentleman wandered about the site a bit and asked the same question of another worker. This one was more willing to talk. He stood up straight and said, with a touch of pride, "Why, I'm doing the best job of stonemasonry in all of England." The old fellow later inquired about the activity of a third worker. When asked, the man stopped, straightened up, and as he stretched the kinks out of his back he tilted back his head and looked up thoughtfully, as if he were studying something which the visitor could not see. He said quietly, "I'm helping to build a cathedral."

This little story speaks volumes about human endeavor. The sad fact is that most people who work for a living feel so far removed from the basic purposes of the organizations which provide their livelihood thay they no longer even inquire about the purposes of what they do. They simply do it. They "take direction." They do as they're told, to the best of their everyday capability. An organization flourishes in its interactions with its environment to the extent that its resources, i.e., the energies of its work force, are concentrated in activities which bring payoffs. Inasmuch as everyone in the organization works for someone, we can say that the ways in which organizational resources are concentrated derive quite directly from managerial behavior.

Because of the enormous range and diversity of human activities, even in the comparatively small organization, and because of the astronomical number of possible communication links which can operate, it is utterly impossible for the organization's managers to regulate all of the activity all of the time. Any one manager's time is divided by a variety of demands, not the least of which are the requests for information and the directions given by his own boss. Each manager has only a certain amount of time and energy available for interactions with employees, and this is not enough to direct their every move. The manager must inevitably settle for a general form of direction, based on whole tasks, whole functions, complete projects, and assigned "missions." He must be content to merely shape, rather than control, their activities. When, for any of a number of reasons, a unit manager does not or cannot give sufficient direction to the activities of his people, then those activities quite naturally take on a kind of randomness. They become to some extent diffused, unorganized, and defocused. Each individual is more or less obliged to figure out for himself what to do — how to spend his workday. The combined effort accomplishes very little, simply because no one knows what is supposed to be accomplished. In some cases, the activity of one person unknowingly offsets or neutralizes the activity of another.

If the work unit has a well-defined "main line" of activity which defines its existence, e.g., processing mail, manufacturing the product, making sales calls, or repairing the office equipment, then the effectiveness of the unit settles down to the sum total of those activities. The remaining activities — whatever they may be — tend to become more and more random, uncorrelated, and nonadditive. If this undirected state of affairs is extensive, and if it prevails for very long, a subtle psychological effect begins to set in. The individuals eventually become preoccupied with the activity itself. They place great importance on "doing things right." There are procedures, methods, and customs for doing things. Life becomes comfortably repetitive, and even though it may be dull for many people, it is essentially predictable. They seldom concern themselves with accomplishment, contenting themselves instead with comfortable activity.

Such an organizational unit may properly be termed an *"Activity Trap."* The people there find themselves trapped — imprisoned in a quagmire of activity, very little of which seems to be accomplishing anything worthwhile, even indirectly. The curious thing about an Activity Trap is that *activity does indeed continue.* Very few organizations, however poorly managed, are at a standstill. Although one might expect that people who don't know what they're supposed to accomplish would do nothing, in fact they virtually always find something to do. This may be unfortunate in one sense, because it makes the lack of direction more difficult to detect. But is also an affirmation of human nature; people try to "do well," even without any direction at all. *People, by and large, want to be active.*

Few organizations are solely Activity Traps. And no organization is so well-regulated and perfectly guided that it has no Activity Traps within it. A typical large organization will have "regions" of its structure which flourish productively, other regions which flounder in the quagmire of activity for its own sake, and still others which function somewhere between these extremes. Activity Traps are not confined to business organizations. Nonprofit institutions, professional and fraternal societies, special committees, and citizens' "action groups" all can fall prey to the activity syndrome. A typical church is an Activity Trap. One finds activities galore—outings, pot-luck suppers, youth groups organized to distract teenagers from the problems and temptations of puberty, policy committees, and choir groups. All these revolve around the Sunday ritual of delivering the sermon and passing the plate. Another typical Activity Trap is the "women's auxiliary"—of almost any kind. A typical professional society will stumble along from month to month with a hodge-podge of luncheon meetings or dinner speakers, with no clear idea of what it should accomplish. A small-town chamber of commerce offers an ideal setting for an Activity Trap. So does the town council.

One basic feature characterizes every organizational Activity Trap: *lack of a sense of direction*. Those in charge of the organization do not *lead* adequately. They do not *teach* adequately. They are unable to provide the "big picture"; the sense of thrust; the grand design which the members of the organization need in order to make sense of their day-to-day activities.

The Amoebic Organization

When an organization's leaders cannot provide its members with an adequate sense of direction, the organization becomes essentially a *reactive* system, simply responding to the sum total of forces acting upon it. Its functioning is similar to that of an amoeba, the small one-celled animal which high school students enjoy watching under microscopes. The amoeba has a very limited behavioral repertoire. It simply drifts along in whatever direction it happens to be heading, until it collides with an object. Faced with this new object in its environment, it either eats it, gets eaten itself, or—failing either of these options—it simply turns ninety degrees and continues on its way. This simplistic pattern of functioning is analogous to the operation of an organization whose members are caught in the Activity Trap. As a group, they drift. Many factors may contribute to this drifting, goalless mode. Sudden and extensive changes in the organization's environment may leave it without a well-defined purpose and mission. Innovative moves by a competitor may suddenly eclipse its strongest product line. A change in legislation may weaken the need for its social service. Often, an industrial firm which has enjoyed a period of economic "boom" will go into a "bust" phase when its hot new product gets old and tired. This may expose the fact that the company's officials were simply capitalizing on good fortune and lacked the capability to give direction to the organization in more challenging times.

The amoebic organization frequently operates in a general state of crisis. Sudden emergencies, major and minor crises, forseeable but unforseen disasters, and sudden unheavals in the workload characterize life in many amoebic organizations. Terms like "brush fire" and "fire drill" become common in the slang vocabulary of its members. Indeed, we could label such an organization a "fire department," with the conscious use of the analogy to a reactive fire station.[6] No manager should take pride in managing a fire department, but many do. Many managers seem to feel a sense of importance and competence in handling crises as they come up.

An amoebic organization often has one or more amoebic individuals at its helm. These people simply react to what they see happening, rather than look ahead to what will probably happen. Such an individual often leads an amoebic private life as well. Amoebic behavior reflects a particular kind of mentality—a philosophy about how to cope with one's environment. The enlightened alternative, which lies at the heart of management by objectives, is goal-directed behavior, reflecting as assertive attitude about coping with one's environment.

The Basic Idea of Management by Objectives

The basic idea of managing by objectives is an utterly simple one, yet probably more managers (and academics) have misunderstood it than have grasped it. Misunderstanding the basic concept usually leads to more of the same bad management and lack of effectiveness which may have led the manager to read about management by objectives to begin with.

[6]Karl Albrecht, "Are You Running a Fire Department?" *Supervisory Management* (June 1977).

Many of those who have published books and articles on MBO have attempted to postulate a *system* — a collection of methods, procedures, rules, forms, and diagrams, saying, *"This* is MBO." In the desperate search for the philosopher's stone — the managerial magic wand — probably a majority of managers have fallen into the trap of conceiving of MBO as a *thing*. They have searched so long and so hopefully for The One Management System that when they stumble onto the basic concept of managing by objectives, they simply cannot see anything but what they expected to see — a system. Indeed, the currently best-known book on management by objectives has as its subtitle, "A *System* of Managerial Leadership." Chapter headings include "The *System* of Management by Objectives," and "Installing the *System"* (italics supplied).

Let's examine the foundation concept of management by objectives. When a manager operates by giving detailed, step-by-step instructions to an employee, the employee depends upon the manager's presence to know what he must do. When the worker finishes his currently assigned task, he must solicit the next assignment from the manager. This mode of operation does not require that the employee know, or understand, or even agree with the basic purposes of the task. The manager simply tells the worker what to do, and by implication he is not to do anything else. This is *management by control*.

But, when the manager takes the trouble to explain to the employee something of the grand design — the big picture he is working on, then the employee can quite readily contribute his own judgement and common sense to do the job well. Further, to the extent that the worker understands the purposes of the enterprise — the objectives — he can continue to some extent on his own. He can pursue the objectives to some degree even without the manager's immediate presence. By explaining the overall objectives to the employee, the manager has liberated himself from the mode of moment-to-moment direction, and has liberated the employee as well. This is *management by objectives*.

This is not a system. It is *not a method.* It is *not a procedure.* It is a concept. It is a philosophy. It is a basic mentality which the high-performance manager brings to the job of managing. Systems and methods and procedures can serve very well to implement the basic concept of managing by objectives. But, the instant the manager mistakes the concept for a system; the philosophy for a method; the mentality for a procedure, he is right back where he started. Chapter 2 discusses and analyzes the principal ways in which managers and theorists have misunderstood the basic concept of managing by objectives.

Many top-management teams have taken off on overambitious tangents after hearing about MBO. Many of these efforts have led to frustration, disappointment, and disillusionment. This has given the term a spotty reputation among practical-minded business managers. Throughout the remainder of this book, the terms "MBO" and "MBO system" will indicate — somewhat critically I confess — the paper-system approach, with its associated *Rigor-Mortis* mentality. I'll use the full term "management by objectives" to refer to the basic concept and its implementation.

Successful application of the key concept of management by objectives rests upon two important suppositions. They are:

1. People work well if their activities have "meaning;" i.e., if they can see and accept some sense of the higher purpose of what they do.
2. Most people will work to achieve objectives if they know what those objectives are, understand them, and anticipate getting rewarded for helping to achieve them.

To the extent that the manager looks ahead, sets reasonable and worthwhile measures of accomplishment, and communicates with employees in terms of this big picture — the desired payoff's — he is managing by objectives.

Some Definitions of Management by Objectives

Writers in the management field have offered various definitions of management by objectives. It may be enlightening to review several of these working definitions.

George Odiorne — "The system of management by objectives can be described as a process whereby the superior and subordinate managers of an organization jointly identify its common goals, define each individual's major areas of responsibility in terms of the results expected of him, and use those measures as guides for operating the unit and assessing the contribution of each of its members."[7]

[7]George, Odiorne, *Management by Objectives* (New York: Pitman Publishing Corporation, 1965), p. 55.

Paul Mali — "Managing by objectives is a strategy of planning and getting results in the direction that management wishes and needs to take while meeting the goals and satisfaction of its participants."[8]

Dale McConkey — "Management by results (sic) may be defined as an approach to management planning and evaluation in which specific targets for a year, or for some other length of time, are established for each manager, on the basis of the results which each must achieve if the overall objectives of the company are to be realized."[9]

David Olsson — "Management-by-objectives is a system whereby the organization objectives are made directional guides for the entire activity. It is a method that focuses attention on, and provides a logical framework for, achievement."[10]

Peter Drucker — "Management by objectives and self-control may properly be called a philosophy of management. It rests on a concept of the job of management. It rests on a concept of human action, behavior, and motivation. It applies to every manager, whatever his level and function, and to any organization whether large or small."[11]

John Humble — "MBO is a dynamic system, which seeks to integrate the company's need to clarify and achieve its profit and growth goals with the manager's need to contribute and develop himself. It is a demanding and rewarding style of managing a business."[12]

Some of these definitions could apply just as well to slavery as to management. None of them, in my opinion, adequately deals with the need to merge the personal needs and objectives of employees with the abstract objectives of the organization. Here is my attempt to state the case from the point of view of this combined payoff:

Karl Albrecht — "Management by Objectives is nothing more — nor less — than an observable *pattern of behavior* on the part of a manager, characterized by studying the anticipated future, determining what payoff conditions to bring about for that anticipated future, and guiding the efforts of the people of the organization so that they accomplish these objectives while deriving personal and individual benefits in doing so."

These various definitions of management by objectives suggest that various writers see the topic from differing points of view. There appears

[8]Paul Mali, *Managing by Objectives* (New York: John Wiley & Sons, Inc., 1972), p. 1.
[9]Dale McConkey, *How to Manage by Results* (New York: American Management Association, 1965), p. 15.
[10]David E. Olsson, *Management by Objectives* (Palo Alto: Pacific Books, 1968), p. 12.
[11]Peter F. Drucker, *Management: Tasks, Responsibilities, Practice* (New York: Harper & Row., 1973), p. 442.
[12]John W. Humble, *How to Manage by Objectives* (New York: Amacom, 1972), p. 4.

to be a consensus of concept, and a consensus on the value of objectives in human enterprise. But there appear to be vast differences among writers concerning the specific means for putting the concept into play. Some writers hold rigorously to the concept as distinctly separate from the methods, systems, and techniques used to implement it. Others seem to see those tangible artifacts as synonymous with management by objectives. The reader of any book on the subject is forced to derive his own "definition," both in theoretical terms and in terms of the practice of managing.

The Cybernetic Organization

After examining many books and articles related to the subject of management by objectives, interviewing many practicing managers (and their employees), and reflecting on my experiences as a middle manager and management consultant, I have concluded that three essential conditions must be present before I am willing to say that an organization's officials are indeed "managing by objectives." I consider these three conditions so fundamental to the application of the basic concept that I have devoted an entire chapter to each one. The three conditions are:

1. *Objectives-oriented managers,* who think in terms of payoffs and priorities
2. *Objectives-oriented workers,* who take an interest in organizational goals
3. *A reward-centered environment,* in which the managers and workers function as partners in pursuing organizational goals

When these conditions prevail, the organization functions as a "non-amoebic" unit, i.e., a *goal-seeking system.* People at many levels, in many functional areas, have a clear idea of the organization's chosen course of direction, and they work in an enlightened way to achieve desired payoffs. And, most importantly, a payoff for the organization brings a payoff—directly or indirectly—to the individual who contributes his efforts toward achieving it.

When the great majority of the people within an organization relate to its leaders in this way, the organization "comes alive." Their activities become more nearly aligned to a common direction, more closely a focused. Such a goal-striving human system may be termed a *cybernetic organization.* The term "cybernetic" derives from the Greek word *kybernos,* which means roughly "steersman." The more closely the organization's people can align their efforts toward a common objective or set of objectives, the more cybernetic their organization becomes. Instead of drifting, they *adapt continuously* to the environment.

From this definition, we can see that cybernetic functioning is a characteristic of the entire human system, not merely of its officials. This is the great potential of management by objectives. If the organization's leaders put the concept of objectives-oriented managing and communicating into play well, they can "turn on" its human capability. If not, then no amount of methodology, no paper system, no procedures, can ever substitute.

Throughout the remainder of this book, this *concept* of the cybernetic organization the three conditions which characterize it, form the foundation for the discussion of *methods* for managing by objectives.

What It Takes to Make Management by Objectives Work

Any manager, at any level, in any organization, can adopt the behavior pattern of managing by objectives. The region of the organization which that manager influences can become a cybernetic unit, if he does his job with a sense of payoff and priorities in mind. Here are some of the key requirements for making management by objectives work for the individual manager *and the people:*

1. The manager should have a clear concept of the purpose and mission of the unit, whether it is a small section, a department, a division, or an entire company or agency.
2. The manager should realistically evaluate the unit's functioning against commonsense standards of performance, on a continuing basis.
3. The manager should think about the future, often enough to anticipate changes and trends which will require adaptive changes on the part of the unit as a human system.
4. The manager should set realistic and worthwhile goals for the organization, usually in cooperation with the members.
5. The manager should communicate these goals clearly to the members of the organization, and prove by his actions that he considers them important.

6. The manager should create an atmosphere of reward-centered goal striving, which enables the members to feel that they receive or will receive something of value as a result of their efforts to attain the objectives.

7. The manager should keep the attention of the members focused on the organization's goals and manage their efforts to help them achieve the goals.

2

Myths and Realities
about
Management by Objectives

Clearly, the term "MBO" is not strictly synonymous with success and happiness in the parlance of practical-minded business managers. For every success story, one can probably find two or three stories of failure— ranging from general dissatisfaction to virtual disaster. It appears that organizational flirtations with "MBO" (whatever the managers of the various units conceive that to be) have not been uniformly satisfying. This chapter describes and analyzes a half-dozen misconceptions—myths, really—which arise most often in the minds of managers who have mistaken MBO for a management panacea. Chapter 10 shows how to recognize some of the more common pitfalls caused by believing these myths.

MBO Is Not a Panacea

Most MBO failures have been marked by great disillusionment on the part of the managers who have tried to remodel their organizations with what they hoped would be a sure-fire cure for whatever problems they faced. Disillusionment is a certain indication of one fatal mistake: *unrealistic expectations*. And the higher the expectations, the more bitter the disillusionment. It is not uncommon for the term "MBO" to become a "dirty word" in an organization whose officials have tried overzealously to make it a way of life. Working-level complaints, a general feeling of frustration with an abundance of paper and procedure, and, finally, general disenchantment typify such an organization. But despite the labels which managers apply to what they do, saying that one manages by objectives does not make it so. Most so-called MBO systems which have ended in disaster were never anything more than a perpetuation of the same old Activity Trap, dressed up in fancy terminology. Trying to install a mechanistic system of directives, measurements, and reporting schemes is not necessarily managing by objectives. But a very large number of managers have been enchanted by the siren song of the "MBO system," and have mistaken it for the long-sought method—the universal cure for management problems. As many managers have discovered to their chagrin, "MBO" is not a panacea.

The Pendulum Effect

The most common result of an overzealous attempt to systematize an organization with "MBO" is the pendulum effect. This is the process by which the organization's managers convert it from a loosely structured Activity Trap to a rigidly structured Activity Trap, hoping vainly that the added structure will bring the hoped-for magical result—improved organizational performance. Typically, a top manager will call in his immediate subordinates and announce, "We're going to start managing by objectives around here. I want all of you to learn about it. You can each start by giving me a list of your objectives for the coming year by tomorrow afternoon." The subordinate managers usually react with confusion and apprehension. They head for the company training library, the city library, or the local bookstore, looking for something which tells them what "MBO" is. They typically conclude that they must issue a variety of measurement-oriented directives to the members of their organizations, and that somehow these directives are to be partitioned and subdivided "down" through their units. This reaction usually tends to spread the feelings of confusion and apprehension down the line.

Next, the top manager begins to wonder how he will know whether the subordinate managers are indeed using the system. So he creates a family of written reports. He directs that every manager, from the first-line level on up, collect the written objectives of his subordinates and send them up the line for compilation. The executive finds it necessary, of course, to appoint a full-time administrator to tend to the planning and reporting process. The administrator dutifully goes around to all of the top-level managers, collecting their lists of objectives and plans, and assembles them into a master document for the top executive. He may even prepare an executive summary, especially since the final report is quite thick.

Next, the top manager establishes a "system" for measuring progress toward the written objectives. Again, there are reports. Again, the administrative assistant dutifully visits the other top managers and collects their inputs. He assembles these into a final report to the top manager. Of course, this is a periodic process, and he finds that he finishes one final report at just about the time he must begin gathering the inputs for the next one.

Meanwhile, the "work" of the organization goes on as usual. The people, including the top manager and the subordinate managers, struggle with the day-to-day activities and demands on their time. In the press of daily business, the "objectives" get more and more out of date, and more and more fuzzy in the minds of the people doing the work. Even the top manager has great difficulty keeping the system going with all the other demands on his time. So far as the people at the bottom of the organizational hierarchy are concerned, nothing has happened—except that their work load has increased. In addition to getting their day's work done, they now must full out "MBO reports." Each year, or each quarter, or each month, they must submit their "objectives" to their bosses. And, again at regular intervals, they must report "progress" to their bosses. They see the "MBO system" as something alien—utterly unconnected with getting the day's work done.

Soon, the managers become dissatisfied and worried about the increasing gap between the original objectives and the performance of their employees (who, after all, are busy doing their "regular work"). They begin to talk ominously of performance appraisals, and of salary adjustments keyed to the accomplishment of objectives. Among the employees, an attitude of confusion, apprehension, and alienation spreads like wildfire. The Rat Race is on.

This course of events, although hypothetical, typifies a great many MBO disasters. The pendulum has swung from pandemonium to *Rigor Mortis;* from undercontrolled Activity Trap to overcontrolled Activity Trap. Figure 2-1 contrasts these two conditions. The organization still has little sense of direction. The members still do not know how to focus their efforts well toward any recognized payoff condition. Where there was a loose, unstructured environment, there is now an environment of procedure and paperwork. People preoccupy themselves with collecting and handing in written objectives, with writing detailed plans, making detailed progress reports, and, of course, revising objectives, replanning, and re-reporting. The organization still drifts. Amoebic behavior is no less amoebic for being systematized.

UNDERCONTROLLED   OVERCONTROLLED
ACTIVITY TRAP   ACTIVITY TRAP

Organization drifts	Organization drifts
Few goals	Few effective goals
People waste energies	People waste energies
Mutually cancelling activities	Paper-oriented, control-
Laissez-faire manager	ling manager
People are busy	People are busy
No one has a "big picture"	Only the manager knows
Few established methods or	the "big picture"
procedures	Many written plans and
No written plans	procedures
Jobs undefined	Jobs overdefined and
	imprisoning

Figure 2–1
Undercontrolled and Overcontrolled Activity Traps

In some ways, the swing from undercontrolled Activity Trap to over-controlled Activity Trap can present an added handicap to the organization. In this *Rigor-Mortis* mode, human initiative becomes locked up within the system of paper work and procedure. The pandemonium mode does, at least, offer some opportunity for initiative and leadership on the part of individuals who want to accomplish more and believe they know how to go about it.

Most "MBO" disasters have their causes in either or both of two basic kinds of thinking traps which befall the well-intentioned managers who catch the fever. They are:

1. Mistaking the basic concept of management by objectives for a cookbook methodology and trying to apply it to a human system which they think of abstractly as some kind of mechanical apparatus.

2. Overlooking the entire matter of employee commitment and assuming that the task is merely to drive people toward a better way of working.

Let's examine some of the MBO myths which arise from these naive assumptions about people and about managing. For simplicity of discussion, the following discussion presents these myths in their extreme form. In many cases, however, they operate subconsciously, playing an unexamined role in the thinking of those who harbor them.

The Cookbook Myth

Myth: "If I can find a good book on "MBO" I'll discover what to do, step by step; I can just follow it and everything will turn out beautifully."

Fact: There can never be a cookbook for managing by objectives, just as there can never be a cookbook for leading a happy life. Books can provide provocative ideas, suggestions, cautions, and systematic tools for carrying out the job of managing. But the essence of managing by objectives lies in the concept itself, not in any procedure. Every manager needs to implement the basic philosophy of management by objectives in his own personal way, fitting his methods to his organization, its problems, its activities, its people, and his own style of operating.

Managing by objectives is not really very difficult. Solving the challenging problems of a particular organization may be very difficult, and an objectives-oriented approach usually helps. But trying to apply someone else's cookbook to one's own situation may be practically impossible. The manager who conscientiously adheres to a few basic principles of objectives-oriented thinking, problem solving, and communicating needs no cookbook. Such a manager relies on his own thinking to help him meet the needs of the particular situation at hand.

The Machinery Myth

Myth: "My organization operates as a hierarchical machine, with up-and-down flows of information and directives. I can operate this machine with full control, simply giving orders and checking to see that they are followed. My organization chart is a complete and adequate description of the functioning of this aparatus."

Fact: Any group of people, from 100 to 1000, to 10,000 to 100,000, constitutes a *social system.* When a number of individuals identify themselves as members of a common organization, they immediately begin to build social networks which facilitate the business of living and working together. They take instructions from those among them who are designated as managers, and they also derive rules for behaving from the larger context of their social system. This happens in groups of all sizes.

A top manager might choose not to pay attention to the social system around him, preferring to deal with the members of the organization as boxes on the chart rather than as diversified individuals, but he experiences the influences of the social system nevertheless. For example, most organization charts do not represent the employee union structure, but it usually exerts a very powerful influence on company management. Military organization charts seldom portray the distinction between officers and enlisted people, yet this social aspect of military life dominates a great deal of the decision making of military managers. The characteristics of the organization's social system are every bit as important as the abstract features of the "formal" organization. Indeed, the commitment of this general population plays a fundamental part in the success in managing by objectives.

The Robot Myth

Myth: "People do as they are told—no more, no less. Unless someone gives them specific instructions, they will simply sit around wasting time. They have no interest in getting the work done, and they have no particular initiative. Their feelings and attitudes have nothing to do with the performance of their jobs. They are here to work, and my job is to see to it that they keep working."

Fact: Each person approaches his role and his job in an organization with his whole self—his skills, capabilities, talents, attitudes, and feelings. He has distinct attitudes about himself, his associates, hiw work, and his managers. These feelings and attitudes color his responses to management direction just as much as his specific job skills and his particular assignment.

When an individual—either a manager or a worker—feels good about himself and his job environment, he tends to work hard to maintain those good feelings. When he feels dissatisfied, frustrated, and alienated from his environment, he tends to seek satisfactions elsewhere. It is the job of the manager to create and maintain an atmosphere in which the worker can find satisfaction of his needs in exchange for working hard and well toward the organization's objectives. Management by need satisfaction operates very differently than management by coercion.

The Jackass Myth

Myth: "People, by and large, are a lazy lot. They don't like work, and they don't want to work. They do their jobs only because they want to make money. If you don't keep after them, nothing will get done. And if you don't check up on them, they'll find ways to get out of working. You can't assume they'll keep working if you turn your back."

Fact: People are wanting creatures. They do the things they do in order to get the feelings and things they want. They want many things — both tangible and abstract. They want creature survival, physical safety, comfort, sexual satisfaction, relief from hunger. They want various articles which make their lives more enjoyable, easier, more satisfying. They want human contact — feelings of inclusion in social activity. They want to feel significant, important, worthwhile. And they want experiences which give meaning and value to their lives. Insofar as money symbolizes the satisfaction of these wants, or leads to the things, feelings, and experiences they want, then they also want money.

The simple fact is that a person will behave in *only* those ways which he believes will bring him things he wants, or which will help him avoid things he doesn't want. If a worker can't imagine a particular type of activity as being associated with something he wants, then he simply won't engage in it, despite the manager's belief that he "ought" to. The managers of an organization can induce its members to behave in desired ways only by providing situations in which the members as individuals can get the things they want in direct exchange for the desired behavior. This great unexploited fact of management lies at the heart of success in managing by objectives.

The Accountability Myth

Myth: "People will only do their work properly if they know there will be a 'day of reckoning.' They must be made to realize that they will be punished if they do not meet the standards of performance set for them by their managers. Without this threat of punishment, they will not take an interest in their work."

Fact: Virtually every "normal" person has a built-in set of ethics—a sense of responsibility. Each person has a highly developed ability to approve or disapprove of himself, as he evaluates his own behavior against his system of values. If the worker accepts some level of performance as appropriate to his values—i.e., it is reasonable and fair—then he himself is the arbiter of his performance. If, for any of a number of reasons, he becomes alienated from the organization and his manager, then he may no longer accept the standard as reasonable. If he believes he is not being treated fairly, then his rationalizing processes may exempt him from the performance requirement or reduce it to the bare minimum.

The manager who falls victim to the Accountability Myth usually overemphasizes accountability (which does, of course, play a fundamental part in management) at the expense of motivation. This manager substitutes threats or implied threats for encouragement and reward. The manager whose thinking is too heavily dominated by this punitive ethic will very likely create a Rat Race in his efforts to make sure no one "gets away with anything." But the manager who bases accountability methods on the assumption that the people will work properly if they are rewarded for it can maintain a healthy, productive atmosphere.

The Visibility Myth

Myth: "To manage properly, I must know what's going on at all levels of my organization, in every functional area, and I must maintain a detailed running comparison between expected performance and actual performance. I must leave no room for human error or carelessness. I must maintain the greatest possible visibility over my organization's processes at all times."

Fact: Any system of visibility should provide for *strategic* interventions by the manager in the organization's processes. A top manager who devotes the same amount of time and energy to stopping pilferage as he does to strategic planning is trying to control the entire organization himself. The simple fact is that all items of information concerning the unit's activities do not have equal importance at any one level. The manager must decide which variables have *first-order importance* for him and his activities as a manager. He needs visibility over those factors, as a matter of effectiveness. He can study second-order variables as a matter of in-depth understanding of his organization, and its internal environment. He should leave third-order variables to those who need to know about them.

The Visibility Myth often leads to a Paper-Mill operation. Frequently, a new manager will demand much more "management information" than he could possibly use, or even understand, in an attempt to get a grasp on the organization's operations. This manager may call for reports, lists of data, copies of various forms, and specially prepared summaries of activities. The "weekly activity report" frequently degenerates into a Paper-Mill process, because neither the manager nor the subordinates are very sure of what the manager needs to know in order to manage well. Generally speaking, the more in touch with the organization and its people the manager is, the better idea he has of his information needs, and the less he must ask for. In this case, a formal visibility system will provide the necessary information without interfering inordinately with the ongoing work processes in his organization.

These six principal myths—the Cookbook Myth, the Machinery Myth, the Robot Myth, the Jackass Myth, the Accountability Myth, and the Visibility Myth—probably account for 80 percent of MBO disasters. By studying them, and the alternative points of view, the manager can develop a clear concept of the requirements for managing by objectives and can select systems and methods which serve his purposes rather than becoming ends in themselves.

3

The
Objectives-oriented
Manager

The objectives-oriented manager thinks and acts in very different ways from the "Fire-Department" manager. While the Fire-Department manager operates *reactively,* the objectives-oriented manager operates *actively.* While the Fire Chief sees himself as coping with a threatening environment, the objectives-oriented manager sees himself as capitalizing on opportunities in the environment. Whereas the fire-fighting mode is a defensive one, the objectives mode is an offensive one. Being objectives-oriented means being payoff-oriented. It means thinking about courses of action in terms of their end products. It means identifying worthwhile payoffs and building systematic plans of action to achieve them. It means adopting a big-picture attitude toward one's own enterprise which gives meaningful structure to one's day-to-day activities. The objectives orientation involves more than just an attitude. It requires a pattern of behavior— a mode of action. We can spot objectives-oriented managers quite easily by looking at the way they go about their everyday business.

Objectives-oriented Behavior

Because he understands the difference between activity and payoff, the objectives-oriented manager frequently asks questions about the *purposes* of various activities—including his own. When an employee proposes a major course of action, the manager helps the employee to clarify his thinking, by asking, "What will that do for us?" They examine ongoing activities from the same point of view, asking, "In what way does this activity contribute to a worthwhile end result or condition?" The objectives-oriented manager learns to ask these basic questions gently as well as forcefully. The manager avoids using such questions as a form of attack, recognizing that, if clumsily employed, they may make other people defensive or even hostile. Instead, he questions in order to learn, to understand, and to clarify.

The objectives-oriented manager communicates with his managerial colleagues in the same way. He proposes worthwhile objectives or cites established objectives and offers courses of action aimed at achieving them. In discussing problem areas with his colleagues, he attempts to identify the payoffs they desire, and only then does he propose actions to provide those payoffs. When he considers a problem-solving group to be straying from its objectives in taking up various tangential issues, he politely invites the attention of the members back to the key issues. For the objectives-oriented manager, a statement of objective is an effective communication tool.

The objectives-oriented manager communicates with his own boss in this same mode as much as possible. He helps the executive to clarify his thinking about the major directions of the organization and to think about additional possibilities. In discussing the allocation of the organization's resources, the manager tries to relate resources to payoffs and to maximize the "cost-effectiveness" of his recommendations. In discussing long-range plans, the manager focuses on objectives as the foundation for the planning process. And he solicits direction and guidance from his own executive in the form of desired payoffs and realistic objectives.

The manager who wants to sell others on a certain course of action begins by selling them on the payoffs. The manager can do this because he himself has developed the proposed course of action by looking at desired payoffs. Only after helping them to understand the value of the objective he is proposing, does he try to persuade them to support the proposed action.

In convincing others to support a project, the objectives-oriented manager tries to place himself in the other person's frame of reference. He applies the so-called "WIIFM?" rule—i.e., "What's in It for Me?"—from that person's point of view. This manager recognizes that each individual needs a feeling of payoff—a sense of reward associated with his efforts in support of the enterprise. He tries to help others find value in the project and to realize that its success will be beneficial to them. If he finds it necessary to compromise, or to revise the plan in order to win the support of others, he focusses on their WIIFM payoffs in deciding what compromises to make. This sensitivity to payoffs enables the manager to specify objectives which others can accept and support enthusiastically.

The objectives-oriented manager continually tests his own ideas against the key payoff questions. When he comes up with an idea he considers a good one, he thinks it through in terms of actions required to make it come true. He asks himself, "What good will come of this? What other benefits might it have? Who will benefit from it? Will they see it as beneficial from their points of view?"

The objectives-oriented manager applies this questioning process gently and positively, rather than in a negative, idea-killing way. He recognizes that new ideas are sometimes fragile and that they may require incubation and further development before they are ready for thorough evaluation. In these cases, the manager conscientiously searches for possible payoffs which might be connected with the new and half-baked ideas. And he grants this same protective support to the new ideas of others.

The objectives-oriented manager works to develop a group of objectives-oriented employees. He realizes that the effectiveness of the organization depends, not on his skill or energy, but on the combined efforts of the people whom he manages. He knows that if they become accustomed to thinking in terms of payoffs, then they will intelligently direct their energies toward worthwhile objectives.

The objectives-oriented manager rewards objectives-oriented thinking and action. He focusses on accomplishment, not on shortfalls. He tries hard to find accomplishments which deserve rewards, no matter how small, and uses reward more often than punishment. Such a manager grants the employees the right to make mistakes, and lets them know he appreciates conscientious effort toward the organization's goals, not merely "a day's work."

The objective-oriented manager creates and maintains a *reward-centered environment* within the organization. By his actions, as well as by his statements, this manager lets employees know that they are working to gain rewards, not to escape punishment. In rewarding objectives-oriented action, the objectives-oriented manager has the courage to grant employees a great deal of autonomy in carrying out their responsibilities.

Autonomy and
Management Style

The extent to which a manager typically grants autonomy to the employees is a key facet of his individual management style. This may range all the way from oppressive overcontrol to a helpless capitulation to group preferences. Clearly, some middle ground is most effective as a general style. The question facing us here is: how does the objectives-oriented manager decide what degree of autonomy to grant?

To understand this crucial aspect of objectives-oriented management, let us call on a simple style model developed by Tannenbaum and Schmidt.[1] For our purposes, we might call it the "autonomy continuum," as represented by Figure 3-1.

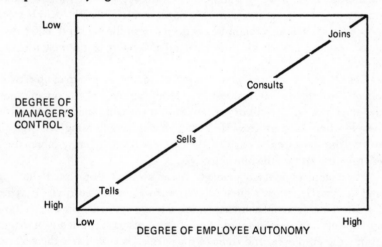

Figure 3-1
Each Manager Has a Characteristic Style of Granting Autonomy

The continuum model clarifies the range of choices the manager has in granting autonomy to the employee. The manager must consider such factors as:

- The individual employee's capacity for self-directed work

[1]Figure 3-1 is adapted from R. Tannenbaum and W.H. Schmidt's Leadership Continuum, which appeared in *Harvard Business Review*, March/April 1958, vol. 36, no. 2 Copyright © 1958 by the President and Fellows of Harvard College; all rights reserved. The Tannenbaum and Schmidt article is "How to Choose a Leadership Pattern."

- The nature of the task itself; the degree of management judgement required; the extent to which it can be freely delegated
- The employee's capabilities for doing the work
- The various choices available to the employee for doing the job properly
- The need for interaction between manager and employee as the task progresses

In some situations, the manager may consider a direct instruction, without further explanation, to be the most appropriate way to get the results he wants. In other situations, the manager may feel quite confident that a particular employee will meet the objective, and feel no need to guide that person's efforts in any specific way. The important factor in this discussion is the matter of *choice*.

The objectives-oriented manager is, therefore, an effective *delegator*. Such a manager learns how to grant autonomy and give direction in the proper balance, for each employee, and for each situation. When the manager delegates a task to one of the employees, he delegates authority as well as responsibility. In holding the employee responsible to meet the objective and obtain the payoff, the manager also has the courage to give the employee sufficient latitude for self-directed action. He allows the employee to plan the course of action, carry it out, and get results, once he feels sure the employee understands the objective.

As Figure 3-1 shows, this balance of managerial control and employee autonomy can vary widely. The objectives-oriented manager needs to be able to vary the balance at will to meet the demands of the situation.

The Importance of Vertical Dialogue

The objectives-oriented manager maintains the proper balance between control and autonomy by means of a free-flowing dialogue with the employees. Such a manager seldom imposes an objective or directs an important course of action without first considering the part the employee is to play in achieving it. He uses time as an asset in achieving the desired payoffs by getting useful feedback from the employee. In a typical conversation, the manager might mention the desired payoff to one of his employees and invite the employee to think over possible strategies for achieving it. He might also invite feedback from the employee concerning the practicality or feasibility of achieving the payoff. Follow-up conversations would then clarify the desired payoff, express it in the form of a specific and worthwhile objective, and arrive at a course of action.

The objectives-oriented manager recognizes the value of delegating the "how to" part of the job to the employee, thereby gaining his support for a course of action which he himself has selected.

The objectives-oriented manager also recognizes that not all good ideas come from managers. He respects the expertise and practical points of view which his employees have and listens with an open mind to their suggestions for new objectives and payoffs. By actions as well as his words, the manager shows that he respects their opinions and their ideas. He keeps his door—and his mind—truly open.

The Right to Be Wrong

The objectives-oriented manager does not pretend to be perfect. He realizes that every manager makes mistakes, gets confused, and makes bad judgements from time to time. He has confidence in his ideas but claims the right to be wrong. The objectives-oriented manager can listen to convincing arguments from a colleague or one of his employees and gracefully change his mind if the facts show that it is necessary.

The objectives-oriented manager is willing to suspend judgements or to consciously delay a key decision if he needs more time to make a better decision. He is frank in admitting he is unsure which course to take and actively solicits decision-making inputs from his staff. Such a manager does not avoid making decisions; nor does he put them off in fear of being wrong. But neither does he make snap decisions just to give the appearance of being "dynamic." The objectives-oriented manager tests his own ideas as well as those of others. He tries new ideas on other people, gets constructive feedback, and rethinks them if necessary. When he is ready for decisive action on a key issue, he will have thought it through, come to an understanding of the payoff factors, identified workable objectives, and developed an effective course of action.

The Future Orientation

The objectives orientation is a future orientation. Figure 3-2 illustrates the objectives-oriented manager's approach in terms of the key behaviors: *look ahead, plan ahead, move ahead.* By adopting a payoff attitude, this manager takes a long-term "process" view of his job. He sees each

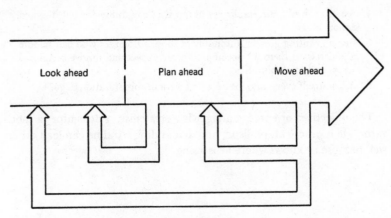

Figure 3–2
The Objectives-oriented Manager Has a Strong Future Orientation

day's work as part of a consistent pattern—a fitting together of the pieces of the puzzle of achievement, a building toward worthwhile future conditions.

This future orientation gives the objectives-oriented manager a measure of control over the organization's destiny. He can anticipate potential problems, and take strategic action to avoid them. And, more importantly, he can seize opportunities for accomplishment because he can see them coming.

Developing an Objectives Orientation

Here are some basic techniques which you as a manager can use to develop an objectives orientation as an approach to your job.

1. Begin asking, "Why?" of yourself and others; "Why should we do this? What's the payoff?"
2. Keep a list of "things to do"; constructively challenge each item on the list; identify the objective you expect it to serve.
3. Make task assignments to employees in terms of payoffs and objectives; listen for feedback and refine your ideas.

4. Assess each of your employees in terms of capability for self-directed action.

5. Begin granting greater autonomy to those employees who can handle it and reward them for accomplishment; expect and forgive occasional errors and small blunders.

6. Ask yourself every day, "Where do I want my organization to go?"

The objectives-oriented manager is a strategist, a delegator, a motivator. He is practical, realistic, and demanding. And he can lead others well because he knows where he is going.

4

The Objectives-oriented Worker

The second principal condition for successful management by objectives has to do with the general population of the organization—the workers themselves. To the extent that the members of the organization adopt the unit's objectives as their own, and work to accomplish them, the leadership provided by the manager is multiplied manyfold. This objectives orientation on the part of the employee is a definite behavior pattern which derives from an underlying positive attitude toward the work and toward the manager.

Employee Attitudes

From the standpoint of employee involvement in the success of the organization, we can classify attitudes as ranging through four general levels:

1. *Alienated*—The "problem" employee; this person feels detached, unrewarded, and perhaps unfairly treated by others in the unit; such an employee may be angry, resentful, and wanting revenge, or may simply feel rejected and unappreciated.
2. *Present and Accounted For*—This person's body and mind are on the job, but his heart is not; such a worker feels he gives the organization

just about what it has coming—no more, no less; he feels there is not much to look forward to and not much to enjoy about his job; it's a place to go every day and a way to make money.

3. *Interested*—This person rather likes his job, and gets along fairly well with his manager and co-workers; such an employee believes in doing a capable job, and takes a constructive attitude toward the organization and its objectives.

4. *Committed*—a relatively unusual mode, in which the employee identifies his personal sense of reward closely with his relationship to the organization; this person may or may not take pride in belonging to the unit, but he finds a great deal about the organization and its activities to interest him and keep him involved.

In any organization various individuals (including managers) will reside at specific levels on this scale of commitment at any one time. Many things can influence an individual's attitude toward his membership and involvement in an organization, but the most common factor, and perhaps the most sensitive one, is the quality of his relationships with his manager and with his co-workers. These are aspects of employee attitude which the manager can influence in a conscious and constructive way.

In this chapter, every observation pertaining to the attitudes of "workers" applies equally well to "managers," who, after all, are workers themselves.

The Manager's Part in Developing Employee Attitudes

A variety of factors, both private and organizational, operate to influence the sense of commitment of any one member of the organization. Private factors such as the individual's own level of maturity, his general sense of self-esteem, events in his private life, and his relative position in the hierarchy, are generally beyond the manager's influence. Within the organizational setting, however, the manager can influence a number of factors which play a part in the individual's commitment to his work.

This chapter focuses on the individual employee, examines the desirable condition of objectives-oriented employee behavior, and shows how the manager can bring it about. Chapter 5 analyzes the broad-scale work environment created by the manager and shows how it influences the members of the unit.

As mentioned in Chapter 1, the manager operates to some extent in the role of *teacher*. Consciously and unconsciously, the manager shapes the attitudes and behavior of the employees. He does this over the long-term course of his relationships with them, as he approves of certain kinds of behavior and disapproves of other kinds. In a very basic way, the manager "teaches" them how to behave in "his" organization. Chapter 5 expands this idea extensively.

The manager can also teach the members of the organization to think and work in an objectives-oriented way. This is one of the keys to gaining the broad-scale participation of the general population to the unit's objectives. By talking in terms of payoff, by modelling objectives-oriented behavior, by discussing problems and assignments in objectives terms, by giving instructions in terms of performance instead of activity, and by rewarding members for objectives-oriented behavior, the manager can develop a pattern of commitment throughout his organization.

Of course, the manager must have acquired the objectives orientation himself in order to teach his employees how to work in a goal-oriented way. Once a manager has made this habit pattern a matter of second nature, he will find it easy to impart it to them. But he must keep in mind a very basic principle of learning: *people will learn and acquire behavior modes which bring them rewards*. The manager must make it worthwhile for them to adopt this new—and possibly unfamiliar—behavior mode. He must systematically and continually reward them for it, psychologically as well as financially. This combination of teaching and rewarding is the only way in which the manager can develop the employee attitudes which result in objectives-oriented behavior.

How the Objectives-oriented Worker Behaves

Just as objectives-oriented managing is a distinct behavior pattern, so is objectives-oriented working. Indeed, the manager is also a worker. What applies to him should also apply to his employees, and vice versa. Let's examine this pattern of goal-directed working.

First, the objectives-oriented worker inquires, as a matter of habit, about the big picture. This employee asks to be informed about the higher purposes of the organization. He expresses curiosity about the organization itself and seeks to know, at least in a general way, where it is going.

When given an assignment by the manager, the objectives-oriented worker asks questions as necessary to clarify the payoff which the manager desires. When appropriate, the worker contributes information and opinions which help the manager to clarify the payoff in his own mind. The objectives-oriented employee habitually "dialogues" his assignments with the manager, making sure they both have the same conception of what must be accomplished.

The objectives-oriented employee demonstrates a standard of performance on his assignments which instills confidence in the manager, and asserts (within reasonable bounds) the right to do them as he sees fit. This employee does not solicit step-by-step instructions from the manager, except in rare cases where the results are extremely sensitive to the method of performance. The objectives-oriented worker takes the initiative in keeping the manager informed of progress on his principal assignments. He offers assurances that he is generally "on track" toward the desired goal and seeks help or redirection from the manager when he is not. When the objectives-oriented employee seeks to renegotiate an assignment, he approaches it in terms of the original goal and deals with the problem in terms of feasibility, priority, and necessary compromises.

When proposing a new course of action or presenting a new idea for the manager's review, the objectives-oriented employee talks in terms of possible payoffs. He shows how his idea will support the organizational objectives. And he discusses the idea with respect to its desirable outcome, not necessarily advocating any one method of accomplishment.

When the objectives-oriented employee discusses problems with his co-workers, he invokes agreed-upon goals as a basis for discussion and negotiation. If the goals become a matter of issue, he concentrates on clarifying and restating them, rather than arguing for a course of action which others no longer support. When clearly stated goals do not exist, such as in special problem areas, he discusses various courses of action with his colleagues, trying to evaluate them in terms of value to the organization.

The objectives-oriented employee actively contributes to the formulation of organizational goals. He offers ideas for improving the organization's functioning, capitalizing on his special vantage point which is close to the day-to-day operation. He keeps the manager informed of new ideas and techniques, as well as developing problem areas.

The objectives-oriented employee is also realistic about the social aspects of living and working in an organization. He accepts organizational politics as a fact of life. He realizes that some managers are less effective, less rational, less aware of human relations, less secure in themselves than others. The objectives-oriented employee does not expect anyone to be perfect, including himself. He takes the typical misunderstandings, communication breakdowns, and occasional interpersonal battles in stride. To be sure, he will find himself caught up in these situations on various occasions. But through the course of his activities in the organization, this employee maintains a sense of accomplishment and payoff. He operates on the conviction that, as a general policy, advancing the interests of the organization is the best way to advance his own interests as a member of the organization.

And, finally, the objectives-oriented worker asserts the right to be wrong, and he grants this right to others. This employee believes that, if he has done his best, he can stand on his record of performance in any organizational environment which has a reasonable atmosphere of leader-member relations. He acknowledges his mistakes and accepts them as a part of being human. The objectives-oriented employee does not blame others, nor does he attempt to cover up his errors. He replans his efforts and takes a new line of attack on the goal he is trying to achieve. He accepts the mistakes of others, and displays a helpful, cooperative attitude in dealing with them.

Job Satisfaction and Employee Commitment

Unfortunately, the pattern of objectives-oriented working will not come about without the proper underlying attitude—an attitude of *commitment*. And that attitude is a very fragile thing. In most medium-to-large organizations in America, alienation seems much more prevalent than commitment. The strength of the labor-management deadlock testifies to the general lack of identification on the part of American workers with the institutions which provide their livelihood.

Commitment is largely an environmental phenomenon. It is an aspect of the continuing process of transactions between the individual and his personal situation. The only reason for working in a committed way would be that one receives direct and continuing satisfaction in doing so. There must be something in it for the individual or he simply will not continue the pattern of work behavior which the manager desires.

In addition to the managerial influences discussed earlier, the individual employee's level of satisfaction with his job—*with the work itself*—can have far-reaching effects on his sense of commitment to the organization. This is one of the most neglected and underexploited facts of human performance known to the management profession. Most of the dull, monotonous, and deadening jobs in American industry have been designed by people who have interesting, challenging, and rewarding jobs. Industrial engineers in particular learn how to design work stations and define work procedures to eliminate or minimize the requirement for psychological participation on the part of the worker. The robotic job design is usually considered the hallmark of industrial engineering effectiveness. Yet it is precisely the element of psychological participation which generates and maintains employee interest and commitment to accomplishment. A dentist once observed, "Every dentist should have his own teeth worked on about twice a year, so he'll understand dentistry from the patient's point of view." We might paraphrase this to say that every industrial engineer should spend about three months or more doing the job he has designed, in order to understand how the worker reacts to it.

In most of our white-collar work situations, the manager has a great deal of latitude in job design. If he studies the various jobs within his organization, he may find many opportunities to redesign them to make them more challenging, more rewarding, and quite possibly more productive. An encouraging trend has been developing in this area over the past few years within the management consulting discipline of *organization development*. This trend is toward "job enrichment"—the deliberate redesign of simplistic jobs in such a way as to call upon more, rather than less, of the worker's abilities and mental processes. Job enrichment usually makes the job more challenging for the worker and gives him a chance to invest something of himself in what he does. This almost invariably results in a greater sense of accomplishment and greater interest in the work. Many studies have shown that job enrichment is a reliable (although sometimes difficult) avenue to greater employee commitment to the work of the organization. In particular, if the employee himself can play a part in redesigning the job, he is much more likely to work wholeheartedly at it.

The Worker as a
Team Member

Another potent source of psychological reward which the manager can influence to a great extent is *team spirit*. For any one individual, a sense of membership—acceptance and inclusion by his peers—can have a powerful effect on his behavior. One who feels closely identified with his immediate peer group, whether it be a working-level section, a department, an *ad hoc* committee, or the top management team itself, will usually go to some lengths to preserve that rewarding relationship. If the group advocates a performance ethic, if its members are primarily goal-oriented, then any one member will tend to behave that way in order to maintain congruity with the group tradition. In this connection, the organization development field has another attractive possibility to offer. The technique of *team building*, which is usually a small-group training experience conducted by an outside consultant, aims to improve the communication atmosphere within the group and increases the sense of personal reward available to each of the members. A well-conducted team-building session has the effect of raising morale rather dramatically, reducing group tension, and fostering a renewal of commitment to the group's integrity and goals.

Autonomy as a
Motivating Force

Individual workers vary widely in the extent to which they prefer to work autonomously. Some people like the assurance of having the manager relatively near at hand to help them over difficult obstacles and to give them assurances about their performance. Others thrive on having a free hand to carry out generally specified assignments and even opening up new areas of endeavor as they see fit. Probably a majority of employees reside somewhere in the middle of that scale. By granting a level of autonomy appropriate to the individual, the tasks at hand, and the situation, the manager helps the individual employee to achieve a rewarding balance between risk and achievement. This sense of autonomy can have a very substantial effect on the individual employee's sense of satisfaction with his job and his overall situation. Probably everyone has seen some person in an organization who blossomed into an enthusiastic, hard-working go-getter when he received a challenging assignment from the boss, along with a special recognition of his status and the importance of his mission. This sense of independent achievement brings psychological rewards so rich and so satisfying that virtually anyone will respond to such an invitation if it seems to offer a reasonable risk level for him.

Self-Esteem as a Motivating Force

It is a well-known but little-used fact that a person will continue to engage in an activity which provides him opportunities to feel good about himself. The term "pat on the back" is common to the vocabularies of most managers, but there doesn't seem to be very much patting on the back in the typical American organization. Praise and compliments given for achievement seem to be more an aspect of individual management style rather than organizational norms. We can safely say that every normal human being wants to feel good about himself; wants to stand well in the eyes of others and so stand well in his own eyes; wants the sense of significance and potency associated with competence and achievement. This fact of basic psychology has direct significance for the day-to-day transactions between the manager and his employees. It points directly to the ecological view of motivation and commitment which Chapter 5 describes. It means that the manager can foster the all-important commitment of the members of the organization by enabling them to find personal significance in what they do. This is not nearly as abstract nor as difficult as it may sound. It means, for the most part, a constructive and humanistic approach to job design. It means placing the individual worker—and, collectively, all of the workers—in job situations where they can experience the sense of accomplishment. This implies, for example, that every job in the organization should be worth doing. It also implies that every job in the organization should have a performance ethic associated with it—that is, the employee should find it possible to do the job well, not just to do it. This notion flies in the face of a great deal of business habit and even tradition, which calls for designing the job around mechanical simplicity and minimum skill, and simply fitting the person into the job. This humanistic job-design concept calls for apportioning the work in an organization—or even reapportioning it if necessary—in such a way that each and every job offers the person who does it a chance to do it well, to be challenged by doing it well, and to be rewarded psychologically by his manager and his peers for doing it well.

One key element of job design which can enhance feelings of self-esteem is *closure*. Closure is the process of completing a task in such a way that one can see a well-defined final result which is of value. It involves responsibility for a complete process, and a chance to get feedback about its successful completion. Unfortunately, the conventional elementalistic approach to job design often eliminates, rather than enhances, this closure aspect. This important benefit of objectives-oriented management is often unrecognized. By communicating the big picture to the employee, and by defining the task in performance terms, the manager offers the employee an opportunity to experience the sense of closure, and to feel good about accomplishing something specific and worthwhile. In many ways, this is the strongest, simplest, easiest, and least costly approach to human motivation available to the manager.

Another simple but profoundly important factor about motivation is that most people tend to work hard and well when their morale is high. And morale in any organization is sensitive to one factor more than any other: the quality of the relationships experienced by the individuals. Managers who make a habit of paying attention to individuals as human beings, in addition to giving them work to do and evaluating results, tend to maintain relatively high levels of morale. The manager who comes around occasionally just to say "hello," or to offer encouragement, or to pass on some good news, is recognizing a basic human need— the need for *contact*. In the lexicon of transactional analysis, this managerial behavior pattern is referred to as freely giving "strokes." One executive calls it "making the 'howdy' rounds." Almost any manager can easily learn this behavior pattern and apply it in dealing with the members of the unit. This one factor may be the most important key to humanizing American organizations in the future.

For the manager who understands these basic features of human behavior, humanistic management comes easy; it makes good sense. The humanistic manager realizes that developing employee morale and commitment to the organization's objectives is important to doing his job effectively, just as the craftsman realizes that sharpening and caring for his tools is fundamental to excellent craftwork.

Whose Objectives?

We need to draw an important distinction between organizational objectives and the personal, private, life-supporting objectives of the individual employee. Why would anyone work in an organization if he could not conceive of receiving any personal benefit from doing so? If he received no money, didn't find the work interesting or challenging, received nothing in the way of friendship or social status from his peers, found the environment physically uncomfortable or unsafe? Clearly, very few people would. Yet, in many situations, managers seem to expect employees to work wholeheartedly and enthusiastically even though very few of these "satisfiers" are available. In some especially toxic environments, money may truly provide the *only* substantial attraction available to the worker.

A simple fact of human behavior is that *no one works "for" an organization or "for" any manager. Each person works for himself*—that is, he works to achieve things which meet his own very personal needs. Only if he sees the organization's goals as congruent with his own will he work wholeheartedly toward organizational goals.

Of course, we must avoid falling into the trap of thinking that the individual needs specific, tangible payoffs every minute of the working day or after every single completed task. This "jelly-bean" theory of motivation is obviously too restrictive for practical application. Every normal human being can use his abstract reasoning abilities to work toward a goal which is comparatively far off. A monthly paycheck, a vacation, or a pat on the back by an executive at the finish of an extended project can all serve as strongly perceived rewards. But the key aspect of objectives-oriented behavior is the underlying attitude of commitment— the feeling that, by and large, "This is a pretty good place (for me) to work." The general feeling that the environment is a rewarding environment rather than a punishing environment seems to be the key to employee involvement and commitment.

5

The Reward-centered Environment

The Ecological View of Organizations

Traditional "mechanical" models of business organizations no longer give us all the answers we need in studying human motivation and commitment. The conventional organization chart—the "block diagram"—developed by Frederick Taylor[1] and his contemporaries around the turn of the century leaves much to be desired in this particular aspect.

Behavioral scientists who study organizational life have been moving steadily toward an "ecological" model of the business organization. This ecological view is dominated not by the subdivision of work processes, nor by the arrangement of tangible factors of production, nor by the abstract lines of command. It includes all of these elements, but it focuses most strongly on the *human system* itself. It recognizes that the radical changes in the nature of many jobs, as well as revolutionary changes in the attitudes of workers toward their work, require that management become increasingly *people-centered* rather than *work-centered.*

Precisely because white-collar work—"knowledge work," as Peter Drucker[2] labels it—has increased in porportion, and because the produc-

[1]Frederick W. Taylor, *Principles of Scientific Management* (New York: Harper & Row, 1913).
[2]Peter F. Drucker, *The Age of Discontinuity* (New York: Harper & Row, 1968), p. 263.

tivity of knowledge work is so difficult to measure, managers must strive to *win* employee commitment, rather than to legislate behavior. This means that understanding human behavior is becoming a necessity, rather than a useful "extra." For American managers in particular, this people-centered view of the human system must also become *individualized*. It is becoming more and more apparent that a specific motivating factor for one person may be utterly uninteresting to another. Enlightened managers are beginning to experiment — with variable success — with individual-oriented concepts such as flexible working hours, individual job plans, and even individualized compensation packages designed by employees themselves within an established framework of benefit options. Treating employees as an undifferentiated mass of statistical creatures doesn't work very well now.

This is a very new trend in American management. Much needs to be learned, and many mistakes will be made. But for the foreseeable future, this ecological view of work and the worker seems to be a compelling and promising trend. A preliminary ecological model of the worker and his interactions with his work environment might look like Figure 5-1.

This ecological model centers on the employee as an individual. It shows the person as bringing needs, values, goals, abilities, and potentials to the job situation. It emphasizes the primary impact of his microenvironment — the physical and social space within which he functions, with its demands, comforts, discomforts, sights, sounds, and sensations as he experiences them.

The job functions also play a fundamental part in this ecological model. The diagram represents these as physically and psychologically "close" to the employee, and exerting a primary influence in satisfying at least some of his needs, aligning with his values, helping him to meet some of his goals, making reasonable demands upon his abilities, and helping him to realize various potentials.

The employee's boss and co-workers play a strong social role in this ecological model of work and working. The employee's relationships with these colleagues can serve as a very potent source of psychological need satisfaction. A sense of inclusion and group membership can have a powerful influence on the individual's behavior in the work setting.

And, finally, the macroenvironment — the general social setting as the employee sees it — offers broad forms of influence on his behavior. The organization as a place to be — an entity to which the employee can

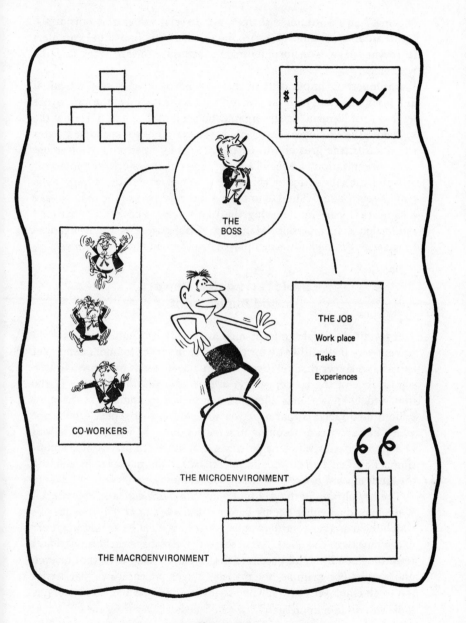

Figure 5–1
The Ecological Model of Work and the Worker

"belong," an institution with recognized social values and purposes—forms an abstract kind of environment which the individual considers to varying degrees in formulating his attitudes toward work and the workplace.

An important implication of this ecological model of the individual and his interactions with the environment is the notion of the employee's level of "involvement" in the organization. From the point of view of the manager, the employee's involvement is a matter of reward. The greater the rewards, the greater will be the individual's personal involvement in the organization as a social system. The objectives-oriented manager operates directly to foster this sense of involvement by helping each employee as an individual to understand the purpose of the unit, to take a significant part in achieving the unit's goals, and to find personal satisfaction in membership. Managing by objectives creates an organizational ecology which fosters employee involvement and commitment.

Basic Facts about Reward and Punishment

A seemingly simple concept such as reward and punishment should present very little difficulty for the typical manager to understand. Yet experience shows that relatively few managers seem to appreciate the significance of the concept of *reward as need fulfillment*. One of the most widely known facts about human behavior, and one of the most seldom used facts, is that a person will continue or repeat a behavior which he perceives as resulting in some condition he wants; and he will abandon behavior which he perceives as resulting in undesirable conditions. This fact has obvious implications for the manager in eliciting the kinds of *work behavior* he wants from employees.

The key phrases in this definition are *"he perceives"* and *"he wants."* If the individual either doesn't perceive or doesn't want the consequences which the manager considers to be rewarding, then he simply won't act to continue those conditions. What seems to the manager to be an obviously rewarding condition may seem to the employee to be irrelevant or even undesirable. For example, the manager might present a five-year service pin to an employee, not realizing that the employee and his co-workers look with disdain upon such "boy scout medals." Wearing the pin might subject the employee to ridicule, rather than foster a sense of pride. A condition is only a reward if the recipient *experiences it* as a reward.

Misunderstanding the dynamics of reward and punishment probably causes more bad feelings, more alienation, and more damage to employee commitment and productivity than any other single factor in management. It seems that relatively few managers have thought through the matter of reward and punishment and have come to a thorough understanding of the difference. For some managers, the power to punish offers the only assurance they can find that they really are in charge. Some managers consider the absence of punishment synonymous with reward. Others "punish" their employees—and perhaps their colleagues as well—in unconscious ways, by critical remarks, demeaning treatment, or unreasonable demands. Some managers seem to consider punishments and rewards as almost tangible forms of transaction with employees, which they mete out with perfect justice from their exalted positions of superhuman perfection.

The following story illustrates one common American view of rewards:

> A country squire living in the deep South was riding his horse one day, and passed along the edge of a cotton field. He noticed a young field-hand energetically picking cotton bolls and stuffing them into a large sack. "Say there," he called. "Looks like you're doing a pretty fine job. How do you like the work?" "Well, I guess it's OK," drawled the field-hand. "What do they pay you for such hard work?" asked the gentleman. "Wellsuh," drawled the lad, "If I does a good job I doesn't git anything. But if I does a bad job they beats the hell out of me."

This individual's perception of the reward system associated with his job probably characterizes more of American work life than we would like to admit. Motivational theorist Frederick Herzberg dubs this approach the "KITA" theory—i.e., motivation by a "Kick In The Ass."[3] This approach to influencing workers is especially common in the "rough-and-ready" kind of job, where supervisors tend to be relatively unsophisticated and uneducated in social skills. Many military small units have this kind of an atmosphere of unquestioned authority and hard work to avoid punishment.

Stout defenders of the KITA theory—known otherwise as "management by fear," "management by baseball bat," or "slave-driving management"— advance a very simple claim: "It works." In the words of the American

[3]For a provocative summary of Herzberg's ideas on motivation, see: Frederick Herzberg, "One More Time: How Do You Motivate Employees?" *Havard Business Review* (January-February, 1968), p. 53-62. For a fuller treatment of the subject, see: Frederick Herzberg, *The Motivation to Work* (New York: John Wiley, 1965).

cynic H. L. Mencken, "The first efficiency expert was Simon Legree." But the proper question is not whether KITA management works, but how well it works. This narrow-minded point of view is not only antisocial, but it leaves out the whole matter of long-term *side effects*. KITA management often does get immediate action, but at the expense of general cooperation or long-term commitment to the organization's goals. Very few punitive managers realize the high price their organizations eventually pay for continuous use of threats and fear as a means of influence over workers. Alienation, anger, frustration, and fear eventually find their outlets, and the consequences for the organization and its managers are seldom pleasant.

Many managers seem to undergo a surprising conversion of attitudes when they receive the first promotion into the managerial ranks. Or perhaps it is a rearrangement of emphasis within their value systems. A person who was an ordinary employee for many years, and who complained bitterly about punitive supervisors who lacked consideration and respect for their workers, may suddenly take on a "Simon Legree" behavior pattern immediately after promotion. Such a new manager, especially one who lacks sufficient self-confidence, may resort to oppressive overcontrol and frequent harrassment of his employees, trying desperately to prove he is "in charge." He may prohibit autonomous action, give instructions only in terms of direct commands, and ride herd on the workers as if he considers them an untrustworthy lot. This "short-memory" syndrome seems very common in business organizations. The effect of the manager's learning process—if indeed he does learn anything—on employee morale can be devastating. In many cases, the new manager's behavior gives rise to employee attitudes and reactions which lead the manager to confirm his insecure world view. The new manager concludes that his employees are indeed uncommitted and unwilling to work. This pathological relationship may settle into a self-reinforcing pattern which continues for years. It may predispose the manager to carry the same attitudes and behaviors to any other management job, and it may predispose the employees to react to the next manager with suspicion and cynicism.

The more enlightened view of human motivation as arising from need satisfaction has been with us for many years. High-performance managers have tested it again and again and proved it works effectively. Let us examine the matter of human needs more closely to see what possibilities the manager has for eliciting the desired work behavior.

Psychologist Abraham Maslow[4] asserted that all of human behavior originates in unsatisfied *needs*. A need, according to Maslow, is an inner demand—an unfulfilled condition, a physical or psychic appetite. The individual behaves in ways which he calculates will result in a reduction of this inner appetite. In this point of view, a variety of needs or appetites usually compete for influence over the person's immediate behavior. Maslow contended that the system of human needs operated in the form of a *hierarchy* or an ascending scale of priority. Certain needs, he said, tend to outrank others and are therefore more fundamental in shaping the individual's behavior. Maslow arranged this scale of needs according to five categories, as expressed in his well-known "pyramid-of-needs" model.[5] Figure 5-2 shows these five levels of needs. Briefly described, these categories are as follows:

Basic Needs—A person's creature requirements for survival and biological well being; air, food, water, proper temperature range, shelter, sexual gratification, physical stimulation, and sensory experiences

Safety Needs—A need for assurances that one's survival is not in jeopardy; reasonable predictability of one's surroundings, which allows one to relax and be free from anxiety

Social Needs—Needs for inclusion in the activities of other people; needs for acceptance and full membership in one or more groups; feedback from group members which confirm one's sense of belonging and significance

Ego Needs—Needs for feelings of significance as an individual; a sense of adequacy and efficacy in one's personal environment; desire for feelings of power and influence; desire to "stand out" among other people as especially significant and potent, as a special person in some way or other

Self-Actualization Needs—needs for abstract forms of personal gratification and affirmation; desire for personal and spiritual growth and development; needs for a sense of "continuing improvement" in one's life; a sense of higher purpose and personal achievement

According to Maslow, Basic Needs demand satisfaction before other levels of needs, as a general matter. Once Basic Needs and Safety Needs have been reasonably well-satisfied for the moment, the individual begins to experience the "pressures" of the other levels of needs. These then begin to shape his behavior more and more, unless or until Basic or

[4]Abraham H. Maslow, *Motivation and Personality* (Harper and Brothers, 1954).
[5]For a highly readable discussion of Maslow's pyramid and other behavioral models, see: Walton Boshear and Karl Albrecht, *Understanding People: Models and Concepts* (La Jolla, CA: University Associates, 1977).

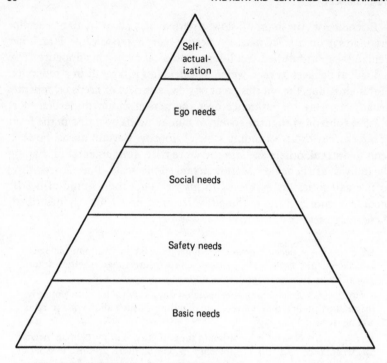

Figure 5–2
Abraham Maslow's "Hierarchy-of-Human-Needs" Model Provides a
Foundation for Understanding Human Motivation

Safety Needs are again in deficit. Of course, a single kind of behavior
or a closely related group of behaviors might satisfy more than one level
of the individual's needs hierarchy. As a practical example, the manager
who feels very hungry, having missed breakfast, will probably respond
more enthusiastically to the offer of a midmorning snack than to the
sense of achievement associated with putting the final touches on a
routine report.

Although the pyramid model does not suggest it very strongly, this
pattern of needs varies considerably from one person to another, and
for any one individual it varies according to the time and the situations
he finds himself in. Human needs are dynamic. They wax and wane
according to the individual's experiences and the outcomes of his behaviors.

Applying this concept of needs to the matter of eliciting effective
work behavior, we can look upon the employee and the organization

as involved in an exchange process, as in Figure 5-3. This shows that the organization more or less "purchases" the desired behavior in exchange for need satisfactions. An important facet of human behavior is the ability to postpone need gratification, or to behave strategically in order to acquire satisfactions sometime in the future. Although this factor is fairly obvious, many managers overlook it in thinking about the work behavior of their employees. Realistically speaking, a great number of the satisfiers which people hope to get by working are programmed for the future. A vacation, for example, may require a person to work steadily for as long as a year in order to enjoy it. In addition, the abstract value of the employee's salary serves as a source of future need satisfaction, perhaps at all five levels of Maslow's hierarchy. The employee realizes that by working at his job (i.e., behaving strategically) he can accumulate tokens which he can exchange with other people for various satisfiers.

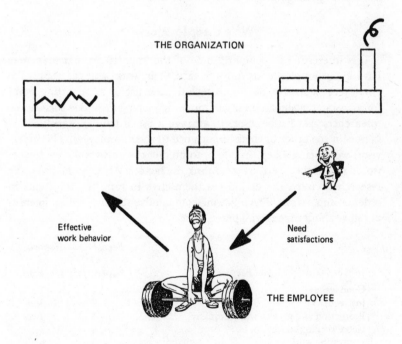

THE ORGANIZATION

Effective work behavior

Need satisfactions

THE EMPLOYEE

Figure 5-3
The Organization "Purchases" Effective Work Behavior by Providing Need Satisfactions

This last point offers an important caution for the manager. In America, we have become so accustomed to earning money by our efforts that we sometimes fail to recognize the organizational setting as a source of need satisfaction itself. If the manager adopts the view that his employees work solely in order to acquire money to use in satisfying their needs away from their job, then he may well overlook some potent—and inexpensive—satisfiers which he has at his disposal. These include simple human interactions such as giving praise, encouraging employees when they try new or challenging experiences, and maintaining a positive social environment.

It has become obvious now that people have many good reasons for working, other than simply acquiring money. There are psychological need satisfactions offered by the human interaction in the work setting which are unique in the individual's life. These are important to the business of managing, and merit further study.

Why People Work

It is interesting to compare some of the impressions that managers have about employee attitudes toward their work with the things the employees themselves say. This technique is useful as a starting point for assessing the climate in organization development. In one such study, researchers asked supervisors to arrange a list of ten "job-satisfaction" factors in the order of their importance to their employees. The supervisors were being asked, in effect, to predict the answers the employees would give if they were asked to rank the factors. At the same time, the researchers asked the employees themselves to rank the ten items in order of importance. The following comparative rankings tell an interesting story about managerial perceptions:

Job Factors	Perceptions of Supervisors	Reports of Workers
Good wages	1	5
Job security	2	4
Promotion and growth with company	3	7
Good working conditions	4	9
Interesting work	5	6
Management loyalty to workers	6	8
Tactful disciplining	7	10
Full appreciation of work done	8	1
Sympathetic understanding of personal problems	9	3
Feeling "in" on things	10	2

In this particular study, we find a remarkable mismatch between what the managers said and what the employees said. Clearly, the manager who considers "good wages" most important to the employees and "feeling 'in' on things" as least important will tend to offer these two kinds of need satisfactions in about that proportion. Indeed, if wages are a once-a-year proposition, subject to cost constraints, the manager may be saying to some extent that he sees himself as not having much to offer the employee in the way of satisfactions. In top-management seminars, I have repeated this study in miniature a number of times. I have asked executives to rank the factors on behalf of their employees, and later in the program I have presented the same list of factors (slightly restated) in the context of a discussion on managerial careers and values clarification. I have asked the managers to rank the factors *for themselves* as individuals. Then I have invited them to retrieve the first set of rankings from their notes and to compare the two lists. In effect, the manager is comparing his assumptions about his employees' attitudes with his statements about his own attitudes.

This exercise never fails to generate considerable surprise and discussion. Managers tend to produce a list of personal ranking very similar to the list given above for the workers in the study. But they duplicate fairly closely the perceptions of the managers cited above in postulating employee attitudes. This generates a very enlightening discussion process about employee attitudes and managerial perceptions. In continuing seminar programs, I have encouraged the managers to present the ten factors to their employees, and to solicit their rankings without any coaching. These provide useful discussion material, and many managers have used them in assessing their organizations as well as their own managerial styles.

You might like to try this survey with the group of people you manage. Simply have the ten items typed in random order on a worksheet. Distribute copies to your subordinates and ask each of them to anonymously rank the factors in order of importance. Don't coach them or in any way "shop" for answers. Before you collect the results and tabulate them, try to predict the outcome. This can be a very humbling experience for a manager, so approach it with a constructive attitude. Survey approaches like these do not, of course, give us hard and fast answers about what employees will actually do when confronted with behavioral choices, but they do clarify the important issue of managerial awareness of employee attitudes and satisfactions.

These findings make it clear that employees as well as managers come to work for a variety of reasons. In an overall sense, making money in order to acquire various need satisfactions outside the organization is probably the chief reason, around which the other reasons revolve. But it is becoming clearer now that a person's work plays a much broader part in his life than being merely a source of revenue. People want to belong. They want to have "a place to go." They want to interact with other people and to receive recognition and appreciation for behavior which is socially valuable. They want the human contact and the sense of personal significance associated with inclusion and acceptance. They want to feel competent—to do things which challenge them within the limits of their abilities, and to conquer those challenges. And they want to grow as individuals.

It is no longer an amazing or outlandish notion that people can find these satisfactions within the work environment. Organizations have all of the possibilities for these kinds of need satisfactions within their structures and within the resources available to their managers. Managers are gradually beginning to grasp the significance of nonmonetary rewards in eliciting the desired kinds of work behavior and in creating reward-centered organizational environments. And because many of these reward modalities cost nothing, managers are beginning to understand the enormous potential of the reward-centered environment for enhancing productivity.

Management Style

The notion of an individual manager's "style" has interested behavioral scientists for a number of years. One of the most respected researchers in this field was the late Douglas McGregor, of the Massachusetts Institute of Technology.[6] McGregor studied a variety of organizational climates and related them to the various interpersonal styles of managing displayed by the key people in those organizations.

McGregor was keenly interested in the differences in employee responses to various behavior patterns on the part of managers. He wondered how some managers seemed able to inspire people—to win their whole-hearted support and their energetic effort—while others seemed only to alienate them and to struggle with them for dominance and influence. He concluded that the differences in these management styles originated in differences in the underlying attitudes of the managers toward the employees as people. McGregor believed that the charismatic managers—

[6]Douglas McGregor, *The Human Side of Enterprise* (New York: McGraw-Hill, 1960).

those who could inspire people—operated on a characteristic set of assumptions about people. He considered this set of assumptions to be a "theory" about human behavior and human attitudes. He believed that a relatively small number of managers subscribed to this theory, while most seemed to hold a very different set of assumptions about people.

The more common theory of management, which McGregor labelled "Theory X," seemed to include the following assumptions about people in the work situation:

1. People don't like work. They find it for the most part distasteful, and will avoid it if they can. They work only to acquire money.

2. Since they don't like work, they must be coerced into working. They must be directed and controlled, and monitored closely to see that they continue to work.

3. People don't like responsibility. They want security most of all, and will not take responsibility unless forced to. The most effective means of inducing them to work toward organizational objectives is to keep them at least minimally anxious about their security.

Some managers will state these assumptions—or opinions—bluntly and forthrightly. Others seem to harbor them more or less unconsciously. But most managers, McGregor contended, manage as if they hold these statements to be essentially true.

McGregor advanced an alternative set of assumptions about people at work, which he felt portrayed human behavior more accurately in terms of environmental influences. He believed that a relatively small number of managers operated according to this theory, which he labelled "Theory Y." According to Theory Y:

1. People want and need activity; insofar as it is a form of activity, what we call "work" is just as natural as what we call "play." The only essential difference between work and play is in the consequences for the individual.

2. People will work toward the objectives of their organization if they receive recognizable rewards for doing so.

3. People will accept responsibility for their work and its results if they are rewarded for doing so.

Each of these two theories leads to a distinct range of possibilities for managerial behavior. According to McGregor, a manager who holds Theory X to be completely true will manage in a watchful, nontrusting, controlling style. A manager who embraces Theory Y emphatically will manage in a very creative style based on human interaction and careful attention to individual rewards.

As a result of McGregor's work, other behavioral scientists have advanced various systems for classifying managerial style. These are too numerous to mention here, but is suffices to say that virtually all of them employ descriptive adjectives to classify style. Terms like "charismatic," "autocratic," "democratic," "consultative," "manipulative," "laissez-faire," etc., abound in behavioral science formulations of managerial style. These make interesting reading and offer much food for thought.

For the purpose of studying management by objectives, however, we need a model for examining managerial *behavior* rather than subjective attributes. Examining the elements of McGregor's two theories, we can identify three key categories of managerial behavior which may be said to define the manager's individual style.[7] These are:

1. *Use of Autonomy*—The extent to which the manager permits and expects his employees to operate under their own self-control, within the context of specific situations.
2. *Use of Reward Factors*—The nature and extent of the reward factors and punishment factors which the manager uses in attempting to influence employee behavior.
3. *Use of Group Process*—The extent to which the manager clarifies roles and responsibilities among the employees, promotes teamwork, establishes and maintains communication networks, and permits group members to influence his thinking.

Each of these three behavioral dimensions can range from negative, pathological patterns to positive and constructive patterns. Figure 5-4 organizes the three elements into a matrix for use in studying various kinds of patterns. Consider, for example, a manager who is rated as granting very little autonomy to his employees, punishing much more often then he rewards, and maintaining only one-to-one communication between himself and the various group members. This would merit a "minus" rating for each of the three elements. Such a managerial style conjures up the image of an octopus, with tentacles reaching out and clamping on to each of the employees, offering very little freedom of motion and very little sense of job satisfaction.

In like manner, we could appraise a manager who grants so much autonomy and so little direction that his employees seldom know what

---

[7]This model was developed by Karl Albrecht and Walton Boshear, in *Understanding People: Models and Concepts* (La Jolla, CA: University Associates, 1977), p. 178. Used by permission.

	NEGATIVE	MARGINAL	POSITIVE
USE OF AUTONOMY	Overcontrol Laissez-faire	Unpredictable	Consistent Individualized Adaptive
USE OF REWARD	Frequent punishment "Stick and carrot" Insincere	Too lavish Unpredictable Rewards not keyed to accomplishment	Rewarding interpersonal style Consistent Rewards follow from achievement
USE OF GROUP PROCESS	Autocratic Encourages politics Abdicates to employees	Inconsistent Wastes time in meetings Communicates ineffectively	Encourages honest dissent Keeps employees informed Uses meetings effectively

Figure 5–4

Three Key Dimensions of the Manager's Style of Dealing with Employees
(Developed by Karl Albrecht and Walton Boshear)

he expects of them; who doesn't punish much or reward much; and who merely reacts to problems as his employees bring them to him. We could describe a manager with these three ratings as "minus, marginal, and marginal." A typical term for such a style is "laissez-faire manager."

In this respect, a strong objectives-oriented manager could be accorded "three pluses" if he stated objectives and delegated whole problems to employees who could handle them; established and maintained a reward-centered environment; and capitalized on group communication processes to keep information flowing, foster constructive controversy, and get employee feedback for his own use in objective setting and decision making.

In considering these aspects of managerial style, we can see the magnitude of the impact which the individual manager's behavior *must* have on employee attitudes and behavior. And we can appreciate the fact that, in a large organization, the general attitude of the work force will derive quite directly from the summation of the behavioral styles of the various managers throughout the organization. If Theory-X managers far outnumber Theory-Y managers, then the organization will almost certainly have a general Theory-X environment.

A well-established fact about organizational environments is that the managerial style of the organization's top manager, and to some extent the immediate inner circle, will be generally replicated down through the organization's chain of command. Managers tend to manage as they are managed. This relationship between managerial styles and the organizational environment is an important key to making management by objectives work.

Theory-X Environments

Theory-X managers create and maintain Theory-X environments, often quite unconsciously. A Theory-X point of view about workers and work leads to a variety of specific managerial behaviors. Many of these managerial behaviors are highly incompatible with the concept of managing by objectives. A pronounced pattern of Theory-X management leads to behaviors such as:

1. A great preponderance of isolated direct instructions to the workers
2. Assigning small, distinct jobs rather than complete "missions"
3. Frequently checking up on workers to ensure that they are doing exactly what the manager ordered them to do
4. Frequent redirection, often accompanied by scolding, reprimands, or other obvious forms of disapproval
5. Prodding workers to do more, do it faster, and do it at a higher level or performance
6. Frequently finding fault, criticizing, blaming, and accusing whenever problems or unexpected difficulties arise in getting the work done
7. Seldom asking the workers for their ideas and opinions
8. Using authority or position power to silence debate, dissent, or controversy about problem areas

These constitute, of course, extreme versions of the Theory-X style of management. Some managers make this a routine style. Others use it as a "fall-back" style in times of difficulty, uncertainty, or extreme pressure. Others adopt it as a partial or occasional style which enables them to cope with what they perceive as personnel problems or organizational difficulties.

Another key factor in the Theory-X style comes from the manager's own feelings of inadequacy and insecurity. A manager who feels uncertain about his own competence, and unsure of the strength of his grip on the work group, may use a domineering style as a cover-up for his feelings. Such a manager may feel anxious about employees "getting out of hand" or about problems which he fears he might not be able to handle. He might believe he can prevent problems by squelching independence and initiative, although he may not recognize that this is what he is doing. The fearful manager may rationalize his overcontrolling style in terms of the supposed inadequacies, laziness, lack of initiative, or uncooperativeness of his employees. And, of course, no manager can stay completely rational at all times, nor can one get completely free of self-serving motives, anxieties, or personal prejudices.

Overcontrol does not, however, form the only manifestation of the Theory-X view of worker psychology. Some managers go to great lengths to coddle employees — to maintain an atmosphere of "one big, happy family." Such a manager may try to cajole workers into doing what he wants. He may ply them with special promises and try to manipulate them into working harder. This is the basic mentality behind a number of incentive programs which attempt to "buy" motivated behavior. Playing music in hopes of stimulating higher productivity often amounts to simply a "soft Theory-X" management method. Playing music to help employees enjoy their surroundings, on the other hand, simply amounts to humanistic treatment of human beings.

In any case, the effect of Theory-X management is generally the same. It produces a sense of imprisonment in the worker. It usually leads to a condition of minimal motivation and psychological detachment. An extreme form of the Theory-X environment produces a widespread attitude of employee alienation, often accompanied by frustration and anger. If the organization also operates at a rat-race level of intensity, this punitive, nonrewarding environment produces strong feelings of anxiety and even overt hostility toward the organization's officials.

Clearly, objectives-oriented employee behavior is too much to expect in such an environment. Motivation, employee commitment, job satis-faction—none of these will take root and grow in the bitter soil of the punitive, nonhuman environment created by Theory-X management.

Theory-Y Environments

Theory-Y managers create and maintain Theory-Y environments usually quite consciously. An enlightened view of human motivation such as this requires a careful, well-thought-out approach to mobilizing human capability. Theory-Y behaviors are highly compatible with the concept of managing by objectives. Indeed, one could say that most Theory-Y behaviors are synonymous with management by objectives.

Typical Theory-Y behaviors are:

1. Praising an employee for a job well done
2. Delegating whole projects or complete problems to be solved; assigning tasks in such a way as to provide "closure" experiences
3. Declaring high-performance standards and expecting employees to live up to them
4. Using authority in a straightforward, nonmanipulative manner, without "apologizing" for being in charge; keeping isolated direct orders to a practical minimum commensurate with the task
5. Encouraging employees to report their own progress on assigned tasks rather than checking up on them; accepting mistakes and problems without reacting punitively
6. Soliciting employee ideas and viewpoints; consulting employees beforehand on matters in which the manager's decisions will materially affect their working conditions
7. Explaining overall objectives and organizational plans to employees from time to time; keeping them informed of new developments which affect them
8. Using group activities such as staff meetings, problem-solving confer-ences, and progress reviews to create a sense of team spirit, cooperation, and mutual reward
9. Encouraging employees to analyze their own jobs and to find ways to do them more effectively
10. Encouraging employees to develop themselves and to seek advancement.

These behaviors form the basic elements of high-performance manage-ment. Note that none of these managerial behaviors involves coddling employees or maintaining a country club atmosphere. A Theory-Y manager can operate in a very tough and demanding way. But the difference between Theory-X management and Theory-Y management is primarily in the use of reward. The Theory-X manager demands high performance and tries to get it with close direction, overcontrol, surveillance, and the threat of punishment. The Theory-Y manager demands high performance and gets it by making it so rewarding that the employees would not do otherwise. There is a world of difference in the eyes of the employee between the demand-and-punish style and the demand-and-reward style of managing. In the Theory-Y environment, management by objectives is almost a foregone conclusion. The employees begin to expect their managers to keep them informed and involved in the big picture. They want to know where the organization is going and they want to know what their individual parts will be in its progress. They work to achieve the goals of the organization for one simple reason: they find significant personal rewards in doing so.

The Group as a Source of Motivation

The ecological view of management and motivation invites us to focus attention on the conditions which prevail in a particular organization as a reflection of the style and methods of its manager. Not only does the group climate indicate the sum total of individual attitudes and feelings, but it provides a very strong form of feedback to individuals. This feedback tends, in and of itself, to shape their attitudes and feelings.

Military leadership traditions offer an interesting point of view here. Hundreds of years of small-group activity have clarified a few simple but extremely important factors which influence individual motivation. Virtually all well-known military leaders have understoof the crucial factor of morale and commitment on the part of the soldiers of their fighting forces. Charismatic leaders such as Wellington, Napoleon, Teddy Roosevelt, Churchill, Patton, and others all devoted great attention to *team spirit* — the individual and collective attitude of oneness. They not only talked about it, they developed it and rewarded it.

Many managers and supervisors preach team spirit to their employees as if it were a matter of obligation. They intimate with their criticism and scolding that a lack of team spirit is the fault of the members of the unit. But they fail to realize that they indict themselves when they complain about the lack of an attitude which is traceable directly to managerial attitudes and behavior. American military commanders often evaluate the performance of subordinate unit leaders by assessing their groups. On the premise that the unit commander has responsibility for everything the unit does or fails to do, they see the commander as a teacher as well as a leader. Four factors constitute the basis for this evaluation:

1. *Proficiency*—The level of attainment of measurable skills, which form the basic capability of the members of the unit to carry out missions assigned to them.
2. *Discipline*—The extent to which the unit's members carry out the tasks assigned to them, voluntarily and with the honest intention to perform well; the extent to which they accept and follow the "rules for living" of the unit as a social system.
3. *Morale*—The general level of enthusiasm and positive attitude on the part of individual members; positive feelings about themselves, their relationships with their peers, and their relationships with their leaders.
4. *Esprit de corps*—A French term meaning roughly "group feeling"—an attitude of belonging; of identification with the unit as a social group; when all or most of the members have this sense of close identification, then the unit "has it."

Perhaps no system of categories could cover all aspects of the effectiveness of an individual organization, because of the large number of environment factors involved, but these four factors seem to go a long way toward diagnosing the manager's influence on the group and its interpersonal climate. Each of the factors stems fairly directly from what the manager does—or doesn't do.

Proficiency, for example, comes from the manager's guidance and teaching, as well as from the employee's education and acquired experience. Any manager can make a straightforward evaluation of the job skills of his individual employees and identify areas of needed development. The manager can then teach the skills himself or arrange for training programs which will help the employees to acquire them.

Discipline derives from standards. The manager can decide quite specifically what constitutes reasonable rules for living and what behaviors these rules call for. He can, by communication and even-handed guidance, maintain this condition of employee discipline in day-to-day activities. Good discipline requires making the code of behavior specific and known to the members of the group.

The manager cannot legislate a condition of high morale, but he can do a number of things to help it grow. He can deal with employees as individuals, trying his best to understand their particular needs, desires, aptitudes, and attitudes. The manager can make his one-to-one transactions routinely positive, rewarding, and pleasant whenever possible. He can tune in on desired employee behaviors and affirm them with recognition and praise. He can give his employees achievable challenges and reward them psychologically as well as tangibly when they succeed. The manager can make *successful work* the norm for the organization, realizing that the satisfaction of doing a job well and being appreciated for it is a powerful factor in building individual morale.

Similarly, although the manager cannot legislate a condition of *esprit de corps,* he can foster it by dealing with the members of his organization as a group from time to time. He can meet with them as a team, discuss problems which face them all, and encourage each of them to offer ideas and suggestions for the good of the team. The manager can keep them informed of upcoming events and changes which will affect them as a group. He can even share his own managerial problems with them to some extent, building a bond of openness and trust with them. The manager can create and maintain a reputation for fairness and nonpunitive dealings with individuals and can reward people for speaking openly and honestly about problems and issues which affect the performance of the group. In these and other ways, the manager can establish a healthy oranizational climate which fosters open and honest communication and which offers rewards to all individuals for cooperation and achievement. The atmosphere in such an organization is virtually electric; it crackles with energy, enthusiasm, and the achievement attitude. When these conditions prevail, no "Simon Legree" manager can even approach the strength and effectiveness of such a unit. For the individuals, their work becomes its own reward. They work hard and well because they get as much from it as they put into it.

6

Analyzing Problems and
Setting Objectives

The managerial skill of analyzing problems and setting workable objectives is, of course, basic to management by objectives. Yet it is probably the most widely neglected process in organizations which attempt to adopt "MBO" as a comprehensive management "system." Most so-called "MBO systems" which have ended in smoking ruins were never more than formalistic structures based on the notion that objectives are like doses of medicine, to be spooned out to the reluctant recipients who will be obliged to swallow them. With regard to objective setting, Paul Mali observes:

> There has been a tendency among managers to regard setting objectives as a relatively simple process; it is deceptively simple, however. The formalization of a statement of objectives requires precision of thinking and forecasting as well as making commitments involving others; most managers are not accustomed to viewing the process in this light. Directing many people in a unified effort to reach a desired end is far from simple.[1]

In this chapter, we will study a basic reasoning process by which the objectives-oriented manager arrives at workable objectives. To do this, it is crucial to establish clearly what is—and what is not—a suitable statement of an objective.

[1]Paul Mali, *Managing by Objectives* (New York: John Wiley & Sons, 1972), p. 110.

Objectives, "Fuzzies," and Goals

Up to this point, I have been using the term "objective" rather broadly, to refer to the desired end conditions which form the basis for the manager's day-to-day work. But in order to analyze objectives and possible courses of action, we will need a somewhat more precise terminology.

Let's continue to use "objective" to refer to any kind of desired end condition, however vaguely or specifically we can state it. Using the term in this way, we can designate as an objective anything from a broadly stated "want" to a very specifically delineated and measureable performance target. It helps to have a general-purpose term such as this, especially in exploring methods for making one's wants progressively more specific and action-oriented. And, since this broad-scale usage of the term corresponds to the typical usage in most business organizations, we can avoid the pitfalls of introducing any special connotation. Next, let's tend toward the term "goal" to mean any objective which we can state so specifically, so concretely, and so unambiguously that virtually anyone will be able to know when it has been achieved. Any statement of objective which falls short of this standard, while it may be very useful as a thinking aid, is too fuzzy and indistinct to point the way to action. Indeed, we can justifiably nickname those kinds of objectives "fuzzies."[2] A fuzzy is an objective which is not sufficiently definite to allow one to recognize its achievement. Figure 6-1 illustrates this relationship among our three key terms—objectives, fuzzies, and goals. Let us now proceed to examine the criteria for each of them.

Fuzzies Are Useful

A fuzzy is a *preliminary* statement of an objective. Many important changes come about because someone first has an inkling of a possibility. For example, a corporate executive might say, "We must defend our product line against technological obsolescence." A middle manager might say to a colleague, "Let's improve coordination between our two departments." An employee might say to his supervisor, "I think we all need a better knowledge of company procedures." In each of these ex-

[2] I am indebted to Robert F. Mager for this useful term. See Mager's witty and thought-provoking book, *Goal Analysis* (Belmont, CA: Fearon Publishers, 1972).

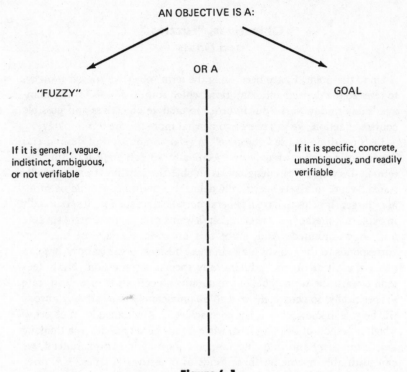

Figure 6–1
Objectives May Range from General "Fuzzies" to Specific Goals

amples, the initial statement is fuzzy. It could be satisfied by an enormous variety of end conditions. It does not specify action very clearly.

Each of these fuzzies, however, can serve as a starting point for a very profitable thinking process. In this sense, we can consider a fuzzy to be a useful communication tool. It calls for a re-examination of the *status quo*. It triggers analysis, evaluation, even controversy. It encourages people to think about the future.

The logical follow-up to a fuzzy is a statement such as "What do *you* think?" or "How might we get a better definition of the possibilities?" The most common pitfall in objective setting is accepting a fuzzy as an adequate goal statement. The only thing "wrong" with a fuzzy is that it does not narrow down the desired end conditions enough. But this in no way diminishes its usefulness in thinking and problem solving

Goals Are Specific

Goals, on the other hand, require much more specific statements than fuzzies. A statement of objective is "specific" to the extent that it suggests action. For example, the statement "reduce the costs of personnel recruiting by 12 percent" may be specific enough for a corporate or agency-level five-year plan. At the working level, it must become more specific so people can decide how to achieve it. The managers who translate this fuzzy into goals might begin by subdividing it according to the major possibilities for action, such as job advertising, selection procedures, and employee retention. Each of these areas would lend itself to a further-disciplined thinking process, which would arrive at more specific statements of objective. As one of the many topics in the daily exchange of ideas within the organization, each of these objectives would become progressively more definite, until the managers and employees responsible for it were satisfied they could make a plan of *action* and proceed with it. By this process, a fuzzy becomes a goal. Quite often a fuzzy will result in several goals, which together represent a desirable result.

Characteristics of an
Effective Goal Statement

An effective goal statement is not fuzzy. It leaves no uncertainty about the desired end conditions. It enables the person who must achieve it to compare various possible actions and to select those which will bring it about. The following characteristics identify an effective goal statement:

SPECIFIC—It spells out, in concrete terms, what is to be achieved, to what degree, and the deadline for achieving it. It uses very specific terms instead of abstractions. It focuses on performance, and it uses performance variables whenever possible. It tells how much, how many, how big, how small, etc. Or, it identifies specific qualitative conditions which leave no doubt as to their attainment.

PAYOFF-ORIENTED—It identifies a set of end conditions which have intrinsic value, or which are associated with something of value. It is clearly a worthwhile thing to achieve; there is an unquestionable element of value in the conditions it identifies.

INTRINSICALLY REWARDING—It specifies a desired set of conditions which will bring rewards *to the person who is to strive for them.* That is, there must be associated with the goal a reward which the "action person" wants and is willing to work for. This may be simply a matter of recognition accorded the action person for achieving it; or it may be a payoff associated directly with the goal. But, in any case, it is only a goal in the eyes of the action person if he himself can foresee a personal payoff in accomplishing it.

REALISTIC—It identifies a target which is reasonably attainable. It accounts for practical experience and various uncertainties, and it allows a reasonable margin for error. It rests upon reasonable assumptions about the future and about the people who will work to achieve the goal.

OBSERVABLE—It specifies a set of conditions which can be detected, a target which can be identified to the satisfaction of all concerned, especially the people responsible for its achievement. These conditions will be clearly recognizable when the goal has been achieved.

These five characteristics, identified by the mnemonic "SPIRO,"[3] determine the extent to which a goal statement will serve as a basis for action. All of them are, of course, relative terms. An objective can range from a fuzzy, which is not very specific, to a clear-cut goal, which is quite specific. Similarly, a fuzzy may be stated without even a very firm idea of the desired payoff; the payoff may become clear as a result of the thinking process by which the fuzzy gets converted into a goal. The intrinsic rewards of the fuzzy—rewards for the action people—may be rather vague and nebulous; they may become crystal clear as the goal statement emerges from the objectives-oriented problem-solving process.

The realistic feature may also be rather vague while the objectives are still fuzzy. Those who first state the objective in fuzzy form may feel unsure of the extent to which it is a realistic thing to strive for; or they may not be sure what level of achievement is realistic. And, of course, the extent to which the achievement is observable may also be open to argument in the beginning. Some individuals might accept a highly qualitative judgement as evidence of an observable objective, while others might consider it too fuzzy to serve as a basis for evaluating actions. Figure 6-2 gives a graphic picture of this useful mnemonic, for quick review.

Every goal statement can, presumably, be made even more specific. One could continue making it more and more detailed, without limit.

[3]John E. Jones suggested this mnemonic. I have modified it somewhat from his original definition. See Pfeiffer & Jones, *1972 Annual Handbook for Group Facilitators* (Iowa City: University Associates, 1972).

Clearly, there must come a point when reasonable people agree that *no further detail will be of benefit to the process of evaluating courses of action.* This is the point at which the goal statement is "SPIRO" enough.

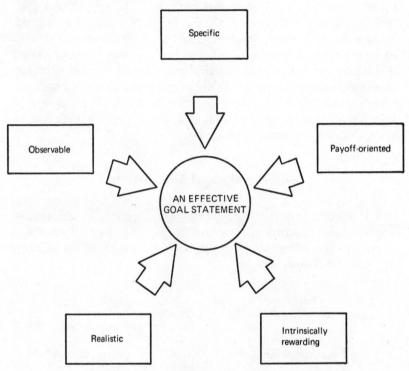

Figure 6–2
Characteristics of an Effective Goal Statement

Two other aspects of the goal statement deserve attention. Both concern the "context" or environment in which the goal statement arises. First, the person who is to work toward the proposed goal must perceive some possibility of an intrinsic reward (the "I" in SPIRO) associated with achieving it. This is frequently an aspect of the situation in which the person works, rather than an aspect of the goal condition. But unless this perceived reward is present, it is unrealistic to expect the individual to work toward the goal. Chapter 5 treats this reward-centered feature of the work environment in depth. For the purpose of this discussion, it is sufficient to remind ourselves that the employee's payoff plays a fundamental part in his objectives orientation. The term "intrinsic" implies that the reward and the goal are, in the worker's mind, inseparable (although not necessarily synonymous). The worker must believe that the reward he wants—recognition, a sense of accomplishment, material benefit, etc.—will come quite automatically as he achieves the goal. In short, the worker must "own" the goal in a very personal way. Second, because we are momentarily considering a goal statement as an isolated result of an isolated problem-solving process, we must remind ourselves that it must not produce any undesirable side effects. That is, its attainment must not prevent the achievement of another goal or set back any other organizational process we consider important. We will need to keep both of these factors in mind as we approach the matter of organizational problem solving and goal setting.

Evaluating Goal Statements

The objectives-oriented manager can use these five criteria—Specific, Payoff-oriented, Intrinsically rewarding, Realistic, and Observable—to evaluate and refine goal statements. Here are some examples of fuzzies and goals for comparison.

Fuzzy	*Goal*
Improve our customer relations.	Complaints and call-backs less than 1 percent by the end of this year.
Increase our share of the market.	50,000 units of product A sold by the end of this year.
Improve employee morale.	Absentee rate 5 percent of working hours or less by the end of the next fiscal quarter.
Improve job opportunities for women.	X qualified women placed in management positions at all levels (in the work-force population) by ———— (date).
Improve our responsiveness to our client agencies.	Work-order response time reduced to less than four hours on Type-A requests, less than sixteen hours on Type-B requests, by the end of this month.

Fuzzy	*Goal*
Improve telephone courtesy to customers who call our office.	Adherance to a courtesy standard; answer within three rings, speak politely and pleasantly, use caller's name, limit "hold" time to one minute, ensure that customer reaches someone who will take responsibility for action; full compliance with courtesy standard achieved within thirty days from now.

Note that in each case, the fuzzy invites further investigation, while the goal more clearly suggests action. Paul Mali refers to these fuzzy objectives as "motherhoods" and offers many sample goals for study.[4] The goal statement does not, of course, specify what to do. But it enables the manager to decide what to do. Also, note that each goal listed in the examples above is only one way to make the fuzzy more distinct. In the planning process, the manager may want to specify several parallel goals which will add up to make the fuzzy come true.

The Management-by-Objectives Problem-solving Process

We have seen, then, that three major phases are involved in thinking one's way from a "want" to its attainment. They are:

1. State the problem or "want" as a fuzzy.
2. Refine the fuzzy into a goal.
3. Achieve the goal by selected actions.

This process might involve a single "sitting" with the problem or it might extend over a long time and many occasions. During the fuzzy phase, the emphasis is on broad issues. The manager thinks in terms of key result areas and tries to identify major directions. He starts organizational dialogues going by stating his wants as best he can. If the manager consciously recognizes this as the fuzzy phase, he need not feel guilty about

[4]Mali, *Managing by Objectives*, pp. 118-23.

stating a fuzzy objective—so long as he intends to refine it into goals with the help of the feedback he receives.

The goal-setting phase becomes a narrowing-down process. It leads to specifically stated, validated goals which the manager and his employees can use as action targets. These goals answer to the fuzzy objective; they form an agreed-upon set of conditions which will fulfill the manager's wants.

The action phase takes its direction from the goal-setting phase. Once the end conditions are clear, the manager and the employees can review the available options for achieving them and settle on a plan which optimizes the use of resources for the level of payoff desired.

We can break down this three-phase process—starting with a vaguely defined problem and arriving at a payoff-oriented course of action—into five distinct steps. They are:

I. Fuzzy	{ 1. State the problem in general terms.
	2. Decide what payoff you want.
II. Goals	3. Spell out the exact conditions which will ensure the payoff.
III. Action	{ 4. List the actions you can take to bring about the conditions.
	5. Select the most promising actions and make a specific plan.

This process may vary according to the problem at hand, ranging from a straight-forward decision (e.g., "reduce operating losses by X dollars this year by discontinuing the ABC product line") to very complex issues requiring careful analysis (e.g., "protect our corporate image of quality and reliability"). In any case, a manager makes a commitment to these five basic steps—either consciously or unconsciously—any time he directs action.

On the other hand, you might find yourself dealing with a problem which requires a great deal of careful thought, and you may decide to spread this objectives-oriented analysis over a long period of time. You might confer with others to get their ideas about how to state the problem more effectively. You may seek alternative ways to put the fuzzy into words. By ruminating on the matter for some time—if, of course, time is available—you might find it possible to frame up the fuzzy concept in a form which permits you to move ahead to establish goals. Breaking the three-phase process down into these substeps may help to clarify your thinking on complex problems. Figure 6-3 illustrates the objectives-oriented problem-solving procedure, as well as the key thought processes involved.

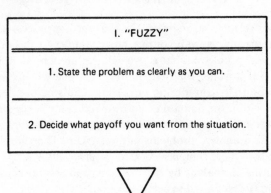

I. "FUZZY"

1. State the problem as clearly as you can.

2. Decide what payoff you want from the situation.

II. GOALS

3. Specify the payoff as a set of end conditions, i.e., the goals you want to achieve by solving the problem.

III. ACTION

4. Identify possible actions you can take.

5. Select the most promising actions and make a plan.

Figure 6-3
The Management by Objectives Problem-Solving Process

Examples of Management-by-Objectives Problem-solving

In order to focus strongly on the goal setting process as a *problem-solving* approach, we will confine our examples in this chapter to the "one-person" problem. That is, we will explore a method by which the manager (or anyone, for that matter) can analyze his wants and set goals for himself, considering only those kinds of problems which lie primarily within the domain of his own action. In succeeding chapters, we shall extend this process to the manager-employee dialogue, wherein both of them analyze problems and set goals. Then we shall broaden that process to more complicated kinds of problems which require "multi-logue" forms of analysis by the manager and several employees whose joint efforts are required to achieve the objectives.

Case #1

The new head of the Office Services Department has discussed his organization's role with the heads of the key "customer" departments and has concluded that the general quality of office service is unacceptably low. Using the management-by-objectives problem-solving process, he might approach the problem in something like the following way.

Step 1: State the Problem.	"The overall quality of our service is below par."
Step 2: Specify the Desired Payoff.	"I want each of my employees to earn the cooperation, respect, and good will of his counterparts in our customer departments by providing friendly, helpful, and valuable service."
Step 3: Spell out the End Conditions which will ensure the payoff (i.e., what you will take as evidence that you have achieved the payoff).	"1. Each employee will have a copy of the service standard for his particular job. 2. Each employee will be able to explain clearly, in his own words, what his service standard is and what he must do to meet it. 3. Each employee will conscientiously adhere to the behavior defined by the service standard, as evidenced by occasional spot checks and favorable feedback from customer department heads.

4. The number of complaints and critical feedback incidents from customer departments heads will be down 50 percent by the end of next month and will be held to an average of less than one per month by the end of the year."

Step 4: List the Various Actions You Can Take to bring about those conditions.

"1. Review the available service standards (if there are any) and update them in cooperation with the key department heads.

2. Give copies of the service standards to the employees of the Office Services Department and allow them adequate time to read and memorize them.

3. Conduct a one-hour indoctrination session with the employees, clarifying any questions and spelling out the basis for compliance. Listen supportively to their concerns about possible uncooperative behavior on the part of customers. Offer constructive suggestions where possible.

4. If necessary, enroll selected employees in training courses dealing with customer-contact psychology and human relations.

5. Brief the key department heads on the new program and solicit their support in getting their employees to cooperate with lead times and other input requirements.

6. Check on progress from time to time and take corrective action as necessary."

Step 5: Make a Plan.

Etc.

This example, although simple, has all the key elements of any major management-by-objectives problem-solving process. It focuses on SPIRO goals and spells out actions designed to achieve those goals. Applying the SPIRO criteria to the goal conditions given in Step 3, we can see that they are indeed specific and measureable; they are payoff-oriented (cooperation, respect, and good will of people from customer departments); they are intrinsically rewarding (satisfaction and good feelings come from improved working relationships); they are indeed realistic; and they are all observable.

Note that the disciplined, step-by-step approach to the problem has the effect of laying it out clearly and simply—perhaps deceptively so. But consider that the fire-department manager might well respond to the "problem" (too many customer complaints or increasing pressure from other department heads) by simply writing a "memo to all concerned." This manager might admonish the employees to work harder, faster, do a better job, and be more courteous. Then he could put the blame on them if the level of service didn't improve. With the objective-oriented approach, the manager keeps his payoff in sight at all times, and spells out very concretely the conditions he wants to bring about. In this case, a wide variety of possible actions becomes apparent. In addition, since the objectives approach focuses on end conditions, the manager can easily monitor the effects of his action to see whether they have brought the desired payoff.

Case #2

The manager of an engineering design group has recently added several new employees and has taken on a broader area of technical responsibility. He now feels pressured, hurried, beset with many small brush fires, and unable to think creatively about the department's goals and directions. Using the objectives approach to problem solving, the manager might approach the problem in something like the following way.

Step 1: State the Problem.	"I seem to have become a 'fire-department' manager. I feel rushed, anxious, and unable to do a good job on anything."
Step 2: Specify the Desired Payoff.	"I want the department to run smoothly, with very few 'crises,' and with our usual standard of technical performance on assigned projects. And I want to be able to relax and think more about the future."
Step 3: Spell out the End Conditions which will ensure the payoff (i.e., what you will take as evidence that you have achieved the payoff).	"1. New Employees will be fully acquainted with their job duties and will be operating autonomously (no more than an occasional request for assistance) within two weeks. 2. We will have an improved work scheduling and monitoring system available to everyone within 2 weeks.

3. I will have an improved personal system of time management for planning my work and setting priorities within 30 days.

4. I will be allocating my time roughly as follows: planning and project monitoring—30 percent; general technical guidance—10 percent; personal counselling and guidance—5 percent; communication with my boss and other department heads—20 percent; unscheduled time for handling new or unanticipated matters—20 percent; "free time" to think about our future direction and generate new ideas—15 percent.

5. I will feel less anxious and more in control of the situation."

Step 4: List the Various Actions You Can Take to bring about those conditions.

"1. Hold a personal/professional counselling session with each of the new employees. Make sure he fully understands his job duties and the department's operation.

2. Assign each new employee to an experienced employee (buddy system), who will provide advice and guidance as the new employee progresses toward autonomous operation.

3. Design and implement a work-scheduling and monitoring system; brief everyone in the department on its operation.

5. Keep track of the amount of time I have available; act assertively to protect at least 15 percent of my time for creative thinking."

Step 5: Make a Plan

Etc.

This example highlights one of the most important benefits of the objectives orientation to problem solving. That benefit is *having a clear understanding of what the solution to the problem will look like.* Instead of simply trying one gimmick or method after another—a typical Activity-Trap mode of operation—the manager in this example first took the trouble to clarify the conditions he was trying to bring about. He began by deciding on the payoff he wanted. Then he proceeded to spell out the goal—those conditions which will assure him of the payoff. After he has done those things, he is in an excellent position to select a worthwhile course of action. You as a manager—or as a private person—can apply this same objectives approach to virtually any situation in which you want to decide how to proceed. You can develop your own procedure for "decision making by objectives," for example.[5] This involves:

1. Selecting the *decision objectives,* i.e., those specific end conditions which the available decision options must meet in order to qualify as "good" choices
2. Evaluating each of the known decision options in terms of the likelihood of its achieving the decision objectives
3. Selecting the one which meets them best
4. Making a plan of action, showing the steps required to implement the selected option and reach the objectives

Similarly, you can apply this thinking process in "training by objectives," using specific desired employee skills as the goals of a training program. The training activities, to be successful, must bring about the goal conditions specified as demonstrable skills.[6]

You can even write an important letter or other document by objectives, by deciding in very specific terms what you want to happen after the reader has finished reading it.

And, of course, "self-management by objectives" offers a very fruitful area of application for the same thinking process. By analyzing your own life and career, you can set realistic and worthwhile goals and go after them systematically.

Pitfalls in Setting Objectives

Setting objectives effectively is a bit of an art. It requires good judgement, flexible thinking, and a sense of the big picture, in addition to the discipline provided by the SPIRO criteria. Most of the pitfalls in MBO applications

---

[5]For an effective treatment of decision making with objectives, see Charles H. Kepner and Benjamin B. Tregoe, *The Rational Manager* (New York: McGraw-Hill Book Company, 1965).

[6]For a thorough treatment of "training by objectives," see Robert F. Mager, *Preparing Instructional Objectives* (Belmont, CA: Fearon Publishers, 1975).

have come from inadequate skill in objective setting. As Chapter 8 shows, workers, as well as managers, must understand how to set goals. Here are some of the typical pitfalls experienced by people deficient in goal-setting skills:

1. *Wrong "scope"*—Attacking the problem at the wrong level, thereby excluding some of its important aspects. For example, a manager might focus on a "problem employee" as if the employee existed independently of his environment and the manager. It might well be a "problem relationship," or a "problem situation"; this would make the goal-setting process very different. Similarly, the original statement of a problem might be, "How can we get the sales of product A back up to its former level?" when better questions might be, "Should we continue to market product A? If so, what changes are necessary to meet the changing market? If not, what alternatives do we have?" This matter of problem "scope" requires careful judgement. The manager must think about the situation and decide how to state the problem in such a way that the management-by-objectives analysis process brings desirable results. Stating the problem too narrowly may eliminate some useful options. Stating it too broadly makes it too cumbersome to handle.

2. *Fuzzies instead of goals*—accepting a fuzzy as a goal statement, in hopes that the typical activity-trap mode will somehow bring improvements. For example, a manager may instruct customer-contact employees to "be more polite and friendly to your customers," with the expectation that they will know precisely what to do. But, in fact, the manager may be able to identify "bad" behavior only when he sees it. He may not have thought very specifically about "good" behavior. He may be surprised to find that some of the less sophisticated employees feel they *are* being adequately polite to customers ("I don't insult anybody. I wait on them promptly. I count out their change, etc., etc.) The manager may need to teach them the transactional skills of stroking, affirmation, and nurturing—skills which are very unfamiliar to many people in our culture. Once he can specify observable forms of desired behavior, he can take action to ensure that the employees learn to adhere to them.

3. *Setting goals too high*—Jeopardizing the action person's perceptions of potential rewards by imposing goals he feels he can't meet. For example, if a manager imposes a cost reduction goal of 40 percent when a feasibility study suggests that this would be the maximum attainable, he is virtually ensuring that the employees will end up with a sense of failure. The sense of shortfall will probably overshadow their sense of accomplishment. If goals are to be intrinsically rewarding, they must be readily achievable. This also applies to the goals the manager sets for himself. If he gives himself a set of goals he can't meet, he will inevitably end up feeling frustrated and inadequate. But if he establishes an overall "portfolio" of goals which do not overtax his time and energies, he will enjoy the sense of a job well done. Reward is more

important than mere effort. Chapter 8 deals with this "achievability" issue more thoroughly.

4. *Activities instead of goals* — Mistaking a specific action for a goal condition. This amounts to confusing the means-to-an-end with the end itself. For example, a manager might say "Our goal is to publish a complete set of departmental policies and procedures by the end of the year." This may or may not be a useful thing to do. If the manager specifies the goal as the condition of having completed this activity, he must be able to show that that condition provides a payoff which he wants. For example if he had started with a problem-statement such as "there is too much confusion about filling out required reports and forms in this department," he could have stated a variety of conditions which might make the problem go away. One condition might be: "Every employee will be able to demonstrate an acceptable working knowledge of departmental policies and procedures — i.e., 'acceptable' for him and his job functions." In this case, the manager could publish policies and procedures as a specific *action* intended to bring about that condition. Or, he might choose other actions such as training or even revising the procedures to make them simpler and easier to follow. Semanticists refer to the word "goal" as a *multiordinal term,* which means that it can designate any of a variety of levels of generalization. We could conceive of almost any "goal" as an "action" aimed at a higher-order "goal." The distinction between a goal condition (ends) and an action statement (means) is often a subtle one, and in this particular example it is a matter for the manager's own judgement. But the objectives-oriented manager is careful not to jump into action until he has assured himself that the action he has in mind will indeed bring about the desired payoff. The manager focuses on payoff conditions until he can confidently select those actions which will achieve them.

5. *Too many goals* — setting too many little goals of minor importance instead of a few major ones. The manager who sets many small goals diffuses his energies and the energies of the employees out of proportion to the value received in return. Chapter 7 deals with the concept of *Key Result Areas* from top management's point of view, and it applies equally well to operational management.

6. *Trying to impose goals on others* — Forgetting that for an individual to strive to achieve a goal, that individual must "own" the goal and perceive a reward associated with it. Chapter 8 deals with this topic in some depth. The manager can readily set goals for his own actions, but if the employee is to work autonomously and in a self-motivated way, there must be a "transfer of ownership" of the goal from the manager to the worker. This is best done by a problem-solving dialogue, rather than by edict. Similarly, if the manager wants one of his co-level managers to work toward a selected goal, he must help that person find value in achieving it.

Learning to Set
Better Objectives

Since objective setting is the heart of the management-by-objectives approach, any manager who is interested in applying it must spend some time acquiring a high level of skill in this area. By intelligent practice, careful thought and analysis, and by continual evaluation of his "track record" as a problem solver, the manager can learn to apply these concepts and techniques effectively. By training himself to think in terms of payoffs, by communicating in terms of payoffs, by applying the SPIRO criteria to proposed goal statements, and by directing his actions toward those goals, the manager can make management by objectives a way of life.

7

Top Management
by Objectives

The "view from the top" of an organization looks very different from that from the bottom or the middle of its structure. Top management, for all its attributes of power and status, is a lonely, uncertain, and very demanding job. Top managers must face and solve problems which threaten the very livelihood of their organizations and people.

We can remind ourselves of the enormous responsibility and accountability of any chief executive by reflecting on the anonymous quotation:

> Experts ranked in serried rows fill the enormous plaza full.
> But only one is there who knows, and that's the man who fights the bull.

In this chapter, we explore the approaches open to top managers in using objectives to direct and guide any large-scale enterprise.

Basic Facts about
Top Managers

In accordance with our policy of keeping in touch with the realities of everyday organizational life, let's review what we know about the people who constitute the inner circle of a typical organization. Here are some fairly important characteristics of typical top managers:

1. They are all, to some extent, political creatures. They have typically reached their positions by a combination of intelligence, hard work, luck, and carefully cultivated relationships with their predecessors and others in positions of power. They pay close attention to the distribution of power and authority within the organization, and they typically guard their own power carefully.

2. They do not "control" the organization; they preside. Rather than manipulate every element of the organization like a puppet master, the typical top manager exerts a direct influence only on his subordinate managers, who in turn influence others who report to them. The typical top manager is acutely aware that his influence on day-to-day "front-line" activities is quite indirect; he usually settles for a strategic form of influence.

3. They are typically men. Fewer than 1 percent of American top managers are women. A large fraction of top managers—perhaps 80 percent—are between forty and sixty-five years old. They bring pre-war upbringing, and to a great extent pre-war values, to the organizational setting. They believe in hard work, achievement, and advancement within the organization as guiding values.

4. They are typically very busy. They work long hours and experience enormous demands upon their time. The typical top manager finds little time to himself—time for reflection, relaxation, or self-renewal. He operates at a fast pace and experiences a high level of emotional and physiological stress.

5. They are usually more intelligent, perceptive, and imaginative than their subordinates assume.

6. They are usually less informed about day-to-day organizational conditions and problems than their subordinates assume. They frequently feel uncertain about decisions they must make, for lack of thorough substantiation of the various decision factors. They occasionally feel confused and somewhat insecure in the face of major changes in the organization's environment, which they find difficult to understand and predict.

7. They have arrived at their jobs by a great variety of career paths; most of them tend to approach management from the bias of individual backgrounds, such as engineering, finance, sales, data processing, legal work, etc.; they are all "lop-sided" to some degree

This view of the typical top manager, as somewhat confused, insecure, occasionally uncertain of his competence in the face of difficult issues, more intelligent and imaginative than his subordinates may think, less informed than he would like to be, and generally overworked, reminds us that the executive job is not simple and that it cannot be reduced to a formula or a cookbook operation. Top managers earn impressive salaries, and they die of heart attacks and other stress-induced diseases at frightening rates. These two facts testify to the complexity and super-human demands of the top-management job. So far as we now know, no system or methodology can replace the top manager as one of the organization's most critical resources. That person's judgement, courage, foresight, social skills, realism, and leadership must serve him well if he is to survive as an executive. No textbook or paper system can do these things.

Yet, ironically, much of the history of MBO seems to be the history of just that—of trying to replace the human skills of the executive with a methodology. Many top managers themselves have yielded to the temptation to try to create "MBO programs" which they hoped would eliminate the uncertainty, anxiety, and stress of their jobs. In most cases these "system" efforts have lead to disillusionment. In some cases they have tended to aggravate the very conditions which top managers have sought to improve. Chapter 1 defined management by objectives as a pattern of managerial behavior. This definition applies to managers at all levels of an organization, including top managers.

The Equilibrium Principle of Human Systems

Most organizations of any size have a fair degree of routine business. Despite environmental changes, ups and downs in business conditions, and the activities of the top managers, most of the organization's people have well-established jobs to do. The proportion of human activity which goes into routine work will vary according to the nature of the organization, its products or services, and its established processes for serving its clients. But regardless of the specific features of its operation, virtually every organization tends to settle into a kind of "equilibrium" condition unless prevented from doing so by outside forces.

Except for those few organizations which experience extreme upheaval, most organizations take on this kind of predictable equilibrium at various levels and in various regions of their operation. A typical large company, for example, will have functions such as accounting, purchasing, personnel record keeping, physical security, equipment maintenance, and food service. As the members of these units carry out their duties over a long period of time, the duties become more familiar, more patterned, and more routine.

Other functions tend toward repeatability and routine as well, although perhaps not without disturbances caused by organizational events. For example, sales activities tend to become well-defined and conventional, unless disturbed by changes in policy, product, market conditions, or management strategy. Similarly, public service activities in a community agency take on a routine character after the employees have worked at their jobs for some time.

For the most part, members of a typical organization prefer this condition of equilibrium, finding a certain amount of comfort and assurance in it. The typical worker likes to feel he understands his job and responsibilities and can carry them out well. Most people like to know what to expect and how to handle the challenges which arise.

This equilibrium principle of human systems plays a very important part in top-management efforts to bring about change. Not only does the typical human system tend toward a well-defined equilibrium mode of operation, but it tends to resist the effects of external forces which act toward bringing about change. Just as the subsystems of the human body act to stabilize its internal temperature, blood chemistry, oxygen supply, and hormone secretions, so the extended human system—the organization—deploys certain corrective subsystems which tend to maintain its internal conditions in the *status quo*. This *homeostatic* feature of human organizations has great significance for management, just as the biological equivalent has significance in the study of medicine.

The longer the organization proceeds without experiencing significant forces acting to change it, the stronger and more resilient these internal "antichange" forces become. Over a period of years, the people within an organization may become so accustomed to certain modes of operation that they have difficulty recognizing the value of workable alternatives. Many times "our way" becomes "*the* way." In many cases this equilibrium may involve healthy and productive modes of operation, and the organization may flourish. But equilibrium can also spell stagnation in many organizations. At times the strength of the equilibrium conditions which prevail within the organization may overwhelm the forces applied by its managers to bring about necessary change. In some cases, the internal pressure caused by the conflict between change and stability can lead to the demise of organizations.

In many instances, the top managers of an organization consider it necessary for survival to bring about changes in its operation. These may range from small procedural changes to a complete rearrangement of the basic elements of the organization. In some cases a top-management strategy of "hold-our-present-course-and-speed" may be a wise one, but more often the name of the game is change. Figure 7-1 gives a convenient pictorial analogy for thinking about this top-management change process. Far removed from the older notion of management as a matter of pulling the levers of a mechanical apparatus, this picture emphasizes the broad nature of the top manager's influence on the multitude of organizational processes.

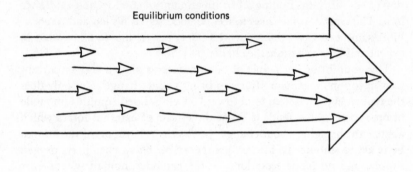

Equilibrium conditions

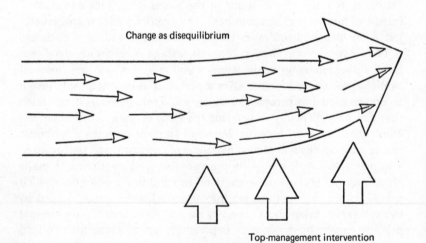

Change as disequilibrium

Top-management intervention

Figure 7-1
Top Management Action Causes Disequilibrium in the Organization's
Ongoing Processes

This equilibrium principle of human systems suggests that any change in the organization's course imposed from above will be essentially disruptive. It will cause *disequilibrium* to varying degrees in various regions of the organization. Some activities will feel very little influence, while others will feel a great deal. The difference will depend upon the nature of the imposed change. For example, the process of adding a new product line to a commercial firm's operation will probably cause great disequilibrium in the areas of sales, engineering, and portions of manufacturing, but little change in areas like personnel, finance, and data processing. On the other hand, a change in the hiring policies concerning minorities will have very strong impacts upon personnel and public relations activities, moderate influence on various first-line supervisors, and little direct influence on activities such as office services, finance, and engineering.

This suggests that making a substantial change in an organization which currently has a strong condition of equilibrium will be somewhat like turning a very large ship while it is underway. Both changes require substantial applied effort, sustained for a considerable length of time. If the manager does not maintain the applied forces for a long enough period, the activities within the unit will very probably return to their former equilibrium conditions. The manager's efforts to change the system must bring about a new condition of equilibrium—one which becomes self-sustaining.

Equilibrium within a human system does not necessarily mean a complete lack of change. Change itself can be a condition of equilibrium. But the nature of the change process will determine whether the organizational forces act to resist it or to facilitate it. Some organizations seem forever in a state of upheaval, where change is strongly disruptive and counterproductive. Others seem so monolithically fixed as to resist virtually all forms of imposed change. A condition of equilibrium-during-change amounts to a "dynamic" (i.e., time-changing) equilibrium.

An example of an organization in dynamic equilibrium would be a company which is expanding at a steady and controlled rate to meet a predictably expanding market for its product or service. Another would be a government service agency which is contracting according to a master plan. Still another would be a large franchise chain which is steadily opening new outlets according to a standard timetable. In all of these examples, the key element is planned and facilitated change. Top managers can facilitate a continuing condition of reasonable equilibrium during a change process by capitalizing on key organizational processes rather than by trying to overpower them. This equilibrium principle plays a very important part in the success of any approach to management by objectives. Many of the disappointing failures of so-called MBO programs have come from overenthusiastic attempts to bring about organizational change too quickly and from underestimating the strength of the resisting forces within the system. The key to making a major change in the organization is to facilitate it by making it attractive to the members, rather than by forcing it on them, and to patiently maintain the applied influence until the desired new condition of equilibrium comes about.

The Environmental "Match"

We can consider the "health" of an organization as directly reflecting the quality of its relationship with its environment, i.e., with the people and organizations who buy its goods or services. A company is usually well-matched to its environment when its customers are buying its services. In good times, the customer demand may be increasing and the company may be growing. In hard times, the demand may be declining or even nonexistent. The company may find it necessary to get smaller in order to survive.

A nonprofit organization (NPO) is usually well-matched to its environment when its services are in demand and its sponsoring sources continue to provide funds. Just as in the case of the industrial company, the NPO's leaders define good times as involving strong or increasing demand and hard times as involving weak demand.

This notion of the environmental "match" provides a convenient linking idea between the notion of "our product" and "our customers." On the one hand, theorists such as George Odiorne[1] contend that the organization's design should center around its products or services. On the other hand, Peter Drucker[2] contends that "the customer defines the business." A useful balance of these points of view portrays the organization's leaders as defining *both* the product and the customer who buys the product in a single creative step. Business history provides many examples of companies with attractive products whose customers simply went elsewhere — to find more attractive products. A good example was the boom in imports of foreign compact cars into America which

[1]George S. Odiorne, *Management by Objectives* (New York: Pitman Publishing Company, 1965).

[2]Peter F. Drucker, *Management: Tasks, Responsibilities, Practices* (New York: Harper & Row, 1973), p. 79.

began in the late 1950s. These practical and economical cars took over an impressive share of the automotive market because the major American manufacturers failed to adapt to changing customer desires. Another example, from the extremely volatile toy market, is the "hula hoop," also a phenomenon of the fifties. While some entrepreneurs got in and got out with impressive profits, others unfortunately overestimated the duration of the demand and went broke with warehouses full of an out-of-vogue product. In the late sixties and seventies, the miniature electronic calculator eclipsed the electromechanical desk-top models, both in price and performance. Some companies manufacturing the previously profitable conventional calculators found themselves caught by surprise.

On the other hand, we find many examples where the availability of a new product or service touched off strong customer demand. The "nostalgia market" of the early seventies typified this. Many people paid impressive prices for horse collars, wood stoves, kerosene lamps, chipped dishes, ship's lanterns, and coal scuttles—trying to catch a wisp of a bygone time of supposed grace and tranquility. So-called "natural foods" made other entrepreneurs rich by providing alternatives to the chemically manipulated American food supply. The audio tape cassette enabled the tape recorder to come of age as a musical product, as well as a generally useful training device.

In practically every case of prosperity or disaster, the one key element was the *match*—that fortunate but temporary compatibility between the product offered for sale and the customer's desires. Some organizations have maintained lucrative environmental matches for years, while others have enjoyed that state of affairs only briefly. Many others, of course, have died aborning because they never achieved a profitable match.

We can sum up virtually all of the fruits of top management's efforts in this one concept—the quality and longevity of the organization's match to the changing business environment in which it lives. Achieving a healthy match and maneuvering the organization's activities to sustain it is what top management is all about.

The "Boom-Bust" Phenomenon

One of the simplest facts of life for a business organization is that sometimes business is good and sometimes it's bad. Sometimes it's very good and sometimes it's very bad. Very few business organizations maintain a lucrative environmental match for longer than three to five years without experiencing at least occasional reverses. Many, many organizations show cyclic patterns of ups and downs, with "boom" periods and "bust" periods ranging anywhere from three to ten years. This "boom-bust" phenomenon stems directly from the less-than-perfect ability of any human system to adapt to a changing environment.

As a general proposition, we can say that whenever an organization suffers a decline in the demand for its products or services (offered, of course, at profitable prices), then its environment is changing at a rate beyond that to which its internal processes can adapt. This view of a company or any other enterprise as a reactive human system, constantly interacting with its economic environment, gives some direct clues about top management as an objectives-oriented process. We might say that the highest-level objective is to achieve and maintain the most profitable environmental match. This calls for a creative, disciplined, thorough-going, and, above all, *continuous* thinking process.

Many factors completely beyond the control of top management can, of course, force the organization out of bounds and into a punishing mismatched condition. A downturn in the American economy, sudden changes in government spending practices, or unfavorable changes in international market conditions could wreak havoc with the economic health of a company. Major changes in state legislation could create upheaval in the environment of a county governmental agency, jeopardizing its budget and its mission.

In studying management by objectives, we must accept these kinds of destabilizing changes as environmentally determined. But in this chapter our interest lies in those factors which top management can indeed control. We need to specify those actions the top management team can take which reliably tend to enhance the environmental match.

How an Organization
Adapts to Its Environment

Inasmuch as any organization is a human system, it deals with its environment in ways which are distinctly and collectively human. Indeed, we run a substantial risk of semantic confusion when we speak of an organization as "doing" anything at all. An organization does not behave in the same sense that a person behaves. An organization is an abstract idea which affects the individual and collective behavior of those who think about it. Let us examine here some of the key human processes which enable the individuals as an "organization" to adapt their activities to changes in their environment.

For the purpose of this analysis, we can identify two very different kinds of change processes. They are:

1. *Reactive change*—Individuals do more of some things and less of others, or they adopt new activities in response to perceived changes which operate "here and now." They change because they must. A supervisor lays off three of his ten employees because his boss instructs him to reduce his personnel costs by 30 percent. His boss did this because the division vice president cut the operating budget by 40 percent, instructing him to allocate the reduction as he saw fit. The vice president cut the budget because the corporate controller told him that sales dropped significantly and his organization had posted a loss. And on and on it goes. Reactive change is a response to *present conditions*.

2. *Anticipatory change*—Individuals modify their activities because they have predicted desirable consequences of doing so. Or they change because they foresee unpleasant consequences of continuing as they have. A marketing executive studies some far-reaching trends in consumer product safety legislation and decides to persuade the engineering department to include certain extra safety features in the product design. The head of engineering decides to launch a design study and a test program to achieve the minimum-cost redesign which will meet the requirements. The head of manufacturing directs a review of the tooling and material-handling processes to anticipate any possible problem areas.

When the primary change mode in an organization is reactive change, its responses to major changes in its environment usually come too little and too late. Due to the inevitable lags imposed by its human communication processes, such an organization continually trails behind the environment. By the time the full magnitude of the change becomes known, the organization's activities may be just picking up speed and shifting in the new direction.

This "internal inertia" virutally guarantees that the organization will become mismatched, unless the environmental changes just happen to favor the match. Sometimes the amoeba happens to be drifting in a fortunate direction. More often, it does not.

Very seldom does the market for a product die abruptly. In most cases, top managers can see the end coming if they choose to look. As George Odiorne notes,

One of the great dangers which any manager, at whatever level, can face is the acceptance of the infallibility of past methods. This is especially true following a period of some success. The empty and decaying textile mills of [the cities of] Lowell, Lawrence, and Manchester along the Merrimack River in New England stand as monuments to managers who thought they could live forever on the fruits of dead men's ideas.[3]

Reactive-change processes typify the amoebic organization. Its muddle-through manager changes only when forced to. In the Activity-Trap situation which characterizes reactive change, individuals try to hold their favorite course and speed, changing only when the deflecting forces bear directly upon them. Reactive change patterns also underly the chronic boom-bust company. During the boom period—which may merely have resulted from good fortune—the company's top managers will congratulate themselves on their cleverness, business acumen, and managerial capabilities. But when the winning streak runs dry—which they probably could have foreseen if they hadn't wanted to believe in "forever"—they blame it on bad luck, the perversity of their customers, economic hard times, or even one another. The fact is that they have simply reacted to the sum total of the immediate forces bearing on them at any one time.

Anticipatory change, on the other hand, characterizes the cybernetic organization as described in Chapter 1. Drucker's "entrepreneurial" top manager reacts to his image of the anticipated future, not merely to the urgent present. No one can eliminate reactive changes altogether, since the immediate future is unknown. Nor will an anticipatory style of adaptation guarantee that the organization will avoid the boom-bust experience completely. But it will assure that boom-bust cycles happen more rarely, and usually with much less severity. It enables adaptation *before* the change, not merely afterward. These two kinds of change, reactive change and anticipatory change, form the basis for the organization's environmental match. Although we cannot completely rule out the effects of fortune, nevertheless we can see that *adaptability* forms the key to the health and survival of any human system. Let us note, with appropriate emphasis, that the adaptive capability of the organization depends almost entirely upon the perceptiveness of its leaders. They control most of the mechanisms by which people carry out their work, and they organize the human resources of the organization largely as they see fit. For the most part, the organization changes only if they perceive the need for change.

[3]George S. Odiorne, *How Managers Make Things Happen* (Englewood Cliffs, N.J.: Prentice-Hall, Inc., 1961), p. 15.

Let's consider a few straightforward examples of reactive and adaptive change. For one, consider a medium-sized electronics manufacturing firm selling citizen's band radios. Its sales performance during the middle seventies is fairly stable and fairly unimpressive, until a consumer buying fad brings "CB" radios into vogue. Over a matter of a few months, orders for its radios begin to skyrocket. Retail outlets exhaust its sales inventory and place rush orders for many more. Six months after the first signs of the environmental change the company has a huge order backlog and its production facilities are taxed to their limit. How does the company adapt to this environmental change? Top management sees this lively new market situation and decides to cash in on it. They expand the work force sharply, going to two shifts and finally three. They buy new production equipment and rearrange the manufacturing flow for greater efficiency. The overstrained facilities are crowded and busy and the pace is hectic. As the boom continues to heat up, the company's top managers congratulate themselves on their business savvy and their managerial capabilities. They decide to expand their facility, step up operations, and capture a bigger share of this delicious economic pie. They acquire new venture capital, lease a large building near the present plant, buy new production equipment, and hire four-hundred new people.

Just as the new plant begins to function fully, approaching its design capacity and turning out radios at an impressive rate, sales orders begin to level off and then to dip slightly. But top management, undaunted, orders an aggressive production program to build inventories and enhance competitive strength on the basis of quick delivery. As sales continue to decline gradually, production continues to increase. As the decline in sales becomes embarrassingly obvious, top management initiates an aggressive campaign of advertising and an expanded sales effort. They hire more salesmen and set up incentive sales plans, while production continues to increase and sales orders continue to decline.

In this imaginary situation, several things have been happening. Competing companies have been taking their own shares of the market. And sales have been declining as consumer demand begins to be satiated and American buyers get interested in other fad items. Sales are now falling at an alarming rate, and it becomes obvious that continuing at the present level of operation will create a dangerous and costly condition of overstocked inventory. A cutback in production means a layoff. It also means possibly closing the second plant and contracting the operation to its original size. This means getting rid of the building and disposing of the new and heavily depreciated equipment. What began as a stroke of good fortune now seems like an economic nightmare. The costs of the retrenchment threaten to overbalance the increased profit from the expansion. With large inventories on hand and sales returning nearly to former levels, production must fall below former levels until stocks decline. Too much of the company's capital is tied up irretrievably in manufactured but unsold products. And here we have the classic boom-bust phenomenon.

This is not to say that top management necessarily did anything wrong or improper. It merely illustrates the consequences of the linear, inertial response lag of the company as a human system. Perhaps its managers could have foreseen the limited lifetime of the fad; perhaps not. At any rate, the organization as a human system pays a very high price for its natural inertia.

Let's consider another imaginary but plausible example. A small community college in California provides a conventional day-time curriculum leading toward an Associate of Arts degree or toward preparation for a full-scale university program of study. The president of the college and the other members of its inner circle have been discussing possible changes which may take place in the organization's environment. Beginning in 1975, they note a buildup in the working-age population within the surrounding community, due to the relocation of several large firms to their area. They also study government statistics on the age distribution of the American population and find that the college-age population is about to decline sharply as the "post-war baby boom" children grow out of the age range typically associated with going to college. The rapid decline in the American birth rate following the baby boom has created a relative shortage of college students, and this implies a coming decline in the college's "sales." Combining these facts with the reported disillusionment of many American young people about the value of a college degree, the top managers of the community college decide to change the organization in anticipation of the environmental changes. They reason that a new educational market is about to develop—that of "continuing education" for young adults. They decide to establish an evening school curriculum keyed to the practical needs and interests of this young adult clientele.

They decide to test the idea with a pilot project. They conduct a preliminary survey within the community and use its results to define a core curriculum for a one-semester test. They establish the program, advertise and promote it within the community, and carry it out for the test period.

Toward the end of the semester, they evaluate the results. Finding them favorable, they then expand the program and institute it fully at the start of the following semester. After a year's experience with the new market area, the college's managers institute a five-year planned approach to developing its role as a community in terms of enrollment, curriculum, facilities development, instructor training and development, and management development for the new evening college. They establish general objectives for the succeeding four years, subject to yearly re-evaluation and confirmation or adjustment. At the end of the first full year, they conduct a thorough evaluation of the accomplishments to that point and ask critically, "Is this still a good idea?"

This is a fairly typical example of anticipatory change—of planned metamorphosis in a human system. Its leaders brought it about by thinking about the anticipated future, defining the payoff conditions they would like to bring about, and giving direction to other members of the organization for making it all happen. This, incidentally, is the same as the definition of managing by objectives.

Emotional Blocks
to Adaptation

In some organizations, certain human forces resist the necessary changes by which the unit must adapt to its changing environment. An understanding of these forces can help top managers to facilitate the changes they want to bring about.

One of the strongest blocks, unfortunately, can be the attitudes of one or more members of the top-management team toward the prospective change and toward the perceived *status quo*. The chief executive, for example, may have such a strong emotional stake in the organization's traditional product or service that he refuses to believe that the world no longer needs or wants it as strongly as before. He may not actively resist a movement toward expansion into other areas, but his lack of active support can often spell defeat for the prospective change.

Factionalism within the top management team can also dissipate their resources and weaken the effects of change processes. For example, a very miserly corporate comptroller can put the brakes on an aggressive program of new-product research and development in many subtle ways. He may see himself as doing this in the best interest of the enterprise, while others may see this as an "antigrowth" pattern of behavior. Similarly, the manufacturing executive may refuse to learn about and try new production methods until the company's competitors are so far ahead that the game becomes one of "catch-up."

And, of course, many an otherwise healthy organization can languish for months or even years while the grim drama of a palace war runs its course. The top-management group may split into two warring factions, each gathering support from investors, employees, or influential customers and clients, waiting until they have sufficient strength to force the others out of the ring. A major government agency may stagnate in the face of a rapidly changing environment, while the chief executive and one or two "hatchetmen" force a second-level executive out of the organization, usually by a long process of paper work, harrassment, and increasing discomfort. The real world of business offers many examples of the kinds of executive power struggles which block the adaptation process necessary for the organization's health, even survival.

Another significant source of emotional blockage is the general population of the organization—the work force. In the case of a union-shop company, the continuing deadlock between top management and the union's managers may present a monolithic barrier to even the most desirable and constructive change. In the case of a nonunion organization, the general level of employee morale and commitment to the enterprise can have an enormous impact on the rate at which a desired change will progress. Some banks and savings-and-loan associations have experimented with extended business hours, including Saturday openings. Most of them have met with general resistance to the idea on the part of their employees. In this particular industry, turnover of entry-level people poses a continuing problem which provides an especially sensitive barometer to employee attitudes. Since turnover means higher cost of operation, the top managers of these organizations must find ways to facilitate the desired changes without creating painful side effects.

Kurt Lewin,[4] one of the first researchers to make a systematic study of human behavior in organizations, referred to the human arena as a "force field," wherein the interplay of various pressures either brought about change or kept the organization in the *status quo*. His notion of "force-field analysis" called for diagramming the major forces operating

[4]Kurt Lewin, "Quasi-Stationary Social Equilibria and the Problem of Permanent Changes." In W. G. Bennis, K. D. Benne, and R. Chin, eds., *The Planning of Change* (New York: Holt, Rinehart and Winston, 1969). See also Walton Boshear and Karl Albrecht, *Understanding People: Models and Concepts* (La Jolla, CA: University Associates, 1977), p. 208.

in an organization, as illustrated by Figure 7-2. In studying the various ways of bringing about change, Lewin identified "helping forces," which act to facilitate the change in question, and "resisting forces," which act to impede the change. This kind of analysis clarifies the major change processes within an organization and suggests approaches managers can use to accelerate a desired change.

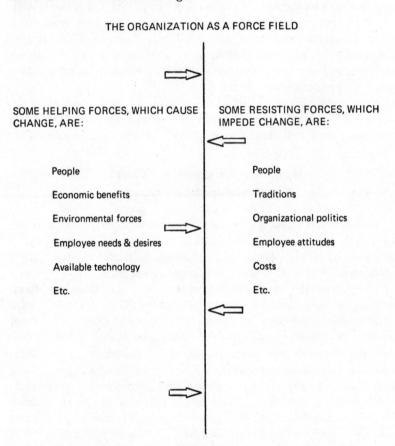

THE ORGANIZATION AS A FORCE FIELD

SOME HELPING FORCES, WHICH CAUSE CHANGE, ARE:

SOME RESISTING FORCES, WHICH IMPEDE CHANGE, ARE:

People

Economic benefits

Environmental forces

Employee needs & desires

Available technology

Etc.

People

Traditions

Organizational politics

Employee attitudes

Costs

Etc.

Figure 7-2
Any Change Process Involves a Force Field of Helping Forces and Resisting Forces

This practical view of the human nature of organizations suggests that top managers must do several things to bring about an adaptive change to meet a changing environment. First, they must have a very clear and specific idea of the change they want to bring about. They must clarify the benefits of the proposed change, and they must be prepared to minimize the undesirable impacts the change may have.

Second, they must combine their ideas and energies and concentrate their organizational resources to make the change come about. They must minimize factionalism and counterproductive personal clashes and develop a strong sense of group commitment to a clearly stated goal.

Third, they must gain the general commitment of the work force to the prospective change by whatever means they can. They must be prepared to compromise, to move at a controlled pace, to re-evaluate the objective from time to time, and to develop employee attitudes which will help the change come about.

And fourth, they must keep their collective attention focused on the organizational processes involved in the change and keep doing the necessary things until the change has become acceptable and permanent.

How Top Management Charts the Organization's Course

The most important single task of top management is to chart the organization's course. It is the job of the chief executive, supported as he sees fit by his immediate executive group, to clarify the basic mission of the enterprise; to state its purpose in operational terms; and to question and requestion the basic philosophies, values, and assumptions which underlie its very existence. Corporate strategy does not result from a single executive meeting planning conference; nor does it stem from a unilateral decision-making process on the part of the chief executive. As a rule, it evolves over time as a result of the confluence of many ideas, opinions, facts and observations, environmental changes, interpersonal influences among executives, and the lessons learned from experience.[5]

We have no mathematical procedure of cookbook process for evolving an organizational strategy. This is a time-extended process which requires human judgement, foresight, analysis, risk assessment, and decision making. Strategy evolves partly as problems arise and as opportunities present themselves and partly through anticipatory thinking on the part of the organization's executives. And it includes a very large measure

[5]For a thorough treatment of top-management strategy, see Basil W. Denning, *Corporate Planning* (London: McGraw-Hill, 1971).

of guess work. But, as Louis Pasteur once observed, "Chance favors the prepared mind."

Charting the course is a distinctly human process, marked by human values, ideas, and opinions, and influenced by the behavioral patterns of the particular group of people who are trying to do it. One of the most significant features of the strategy-setting process is the relative balance of the individual personalities involved. An outspoken executive, even though poorly informed, can often gain support for his values and opinions, in opposition to a more mild-mannered person who may be better informed and able to substantiate his views more effectively if given a chance. Similarly, those who do not hold strong opinions on a particular matter may find themselves going along with the most forceful advocate of one of the several points of view. At times, this "group-think" process can limit the effectiveness of the top-management team in exploring a wide range of possibilities. In other cases, the diversity of views and attitudes can enrich the process of exploration. The personal communication skills of the chief executive officer play an extremely important part in the effectiveness of the top-management group's idea exchange. Another fundamental factor in charting the organization's course is the simple matter of its present course. Any organization except one which is floundering helplessly will have a general momentum in some direction or other. This may be an upward momentum in the direction of expanding sales or income. Or it may be a downward one in the direction of shrinkage and retrenchment.

In any case, the momentum of the current organizational course will have a powerful effect on the thinking of its top managers. Very seldom does a top-management team decide to bring about a wholesale redefinition of the organization's course. Usually, they take the present course and speed as a point of departure for planned change to meet the environmental changes they can foresee.

In this sense, top management can usually be said to "rechart" the course, rather than to chart it in any original sense. The landscape for this navigation process consists of a mixture of the present state of affairs, upcoming problems, perceived opportunities, and conjectures about eventual possibilities. Charting the course is somewhat analogous to deciding "where the action will be" and considering the time required to get there. Another useful navigation analogy is that of sending a space vehicle to the moon or to any other heavenly body. When the crew of the Apollo 11 project set out to go to the moon, they did not aim at the moon. Instead, they navigated to the place where they expected the moon to be, accounting for their own travel time and the predicted course of the moon in its orbit. Organizational strategy setting is strongly analogous to this spatial navigation process.

According to Peter F. Drucker, setting the organization's strategy amounts to finding *meaningful and satisfying* answers to the question "What is our business?"[6] Associated questions include: "If we ourselves do nothing to change it, what will it become?" and "What *should* it be?" Drucker contends that top management must find a clear and unequivocal statement of the basic purpose and mission of the enterprise, in terms of its customers, its source of economic survival, and growth. This is equivalent to defining its environmental match as discussed previously in this chapter.

For any particular organization, the answer to "What is our business?" can range from simply "more of the same," in a case where the organization has locked on to a hot new product or a strongly demanded service, all the way to an agonizing search for a basic identity. In any case, the question does confront the top management team time and time again, and they must step up to it.

Although we have no mathematical procedure for deriving an organizational strategy, we can indeed define a few basic steps which top managers must take if they are to do the job effectively. They must:

1. Evaluate the current state of the organization's environmental match.
2. Study the organization's environment and detect important trends and change processes.
3. Specify the nature of the environmental match they want the organization to have in the future and the strategic organizational "thrust" necessary to bring it about.
4. Set goals which spell out the desired end conditions for a selected point (or points) in time.
5. Decide what actions and organizational changes are necessary to achieve the new goals and make a strategic plan for achieving them.

Let's consider these general steps in greater depth. Evaluation of present status probably offers the least challenge of any of the five steps. Most top managers are acutely aware of how well their organizations are doing, usually in comparison to past performance. In some cases,

[6]Drucker, *Management: Tasks, Responsibilities, Practices*, p. 79.

however, they may consider too small a picture of their environmental match, such as limiting their attention to profit and loss figures or to a few conventional measures of service quality. In assessing the quality of the current environmental match, top managers should consider factors such as:

1. Gross income
2. Profit
3. Product or service volume
4. Product or service quality levels (customer-derived)
5. Customer attitudes toward the organization
6. Competitive stance
7. General reputation or image of the organization
8. Any special problem situations
9. Any special advantages or favorable situations
10. Positive or negative historical trends in the above factors

This must be a comprehensive and honest assessment. It must focus on present conditions and the apparent direction of the trends which those conditions indicate. Slavish attention to the "bottom line" of the balance sheet and operating statement is a very myopic style of assessment which overlooks a number of other important performance dimensions. The bottom-line view is important, but the top-management team needs a much more comprehensive and specific assessment.

The second step in the strategic process, studying the environment, is perhaps the most challenging and the most critical to long-term performance and health. The environmental match which the organization enjoys (or suffers) today is a result of the management thinking processes and decisions of three to five years ago. Conversely, top management's attention to the perceived environmental trends of today will return a payoff over many years to come.

Assessing the Environment

Studying the organization's environment amounts to asking the question, "What's happening that may be important to our organization?" Top managers can understand the composite environment more easily by analyzing a variety of "subenvironments." This point of view suggests that the organization experiences a wide variety of external influences,

all superimposed in their impact on its internal processes. Some of the
major kinds of environments are:

1. *The Economic Environment* — The general state of the American
economy, state and local economic conditions, and the health of the
specific economic sector within which the organization does business;
world economic conditions, if they exert a significant influence on
the organization; the availability of capital; the general level of dis-
posable consumer income, or the strength of the spending power of
institutional customers who buy the products or services; budgetary
processes within the parent organization, if any; government spending
trends.

2. *The Customer Environment* — Current activities of customers, either
individual consumers or organizations which buy the products or services
(this includes the client population in the case of a social service organization); what they are saying and what they are doing; what other
products or services they currently buy; their apparent attitudes toward
the organization and its product line; their demographic makeup, i.e.,
their ages, family status, income levels, living conditions, education,
occupations, etc.; apparent changes in their spending habits; behavior
which indicates any currently unsatisfied needs or wants.

3. *The Competitive Environment* — Activities and trends among other
organizations which offer competing products and services to the customer
community; new products they have developed; apparent intentions
to change their images, open new-market areas, encroach on existing
areas, or abandon currently active areas; trends in the advertising
activities of the competitors; relative degree of customer acceptance
of competitor products and new ideas; major investments in capital
equipment, research, product development, or imagebuilding which
suggest long-term commitment of the competitor's resources and continued
thrust in a particular direction.

4. *The Technological Environment* — The availability of new industrial
processes, materials, techniques, components, or subsystems, which
will enable the organization or its competitors to offer products or services
which are new, better, or cheaper than those presently available; technological changes within the society which may render obsolete some of
the organization's products or services by providing gross conceptual
alternatives (for example the possibility of reducing executive travel by
long-distance television communication); technological changes brought
about by concentrated effort on the part of government agencies or
large corporations having a stake in particular technical areas.

5. *The Legal Environment* — Trends in legislation or enforcement (case
law, court decision, etc.) which may jeopardize the value of the organization's products or services to its customers; efforts of federal, state,
or local government agencies to change business practices; positions
taken by prominent lawmakers on issues of importance to the organization's business.

6. *The Social Environment* — Trends in attitudes and values in the society which may affect the organization's relationships with its customers; social movements which may influence the attitudes and behavior of the organization's work force; apparent increase or decrease in the attractiveness of the organization's general product line to customers; demographic changes, such as population trends, family mobility, educational pursuits, etc. which may increase or decrease demand; current or prospective fads which may affect customer behavior; social processes which can be expected to present problems which the organization's products or services can solve.

7. *The Political Environment* — Major trends and forces among governmental agencies and personalities which influence the organization directly or indirectly; legislative policy or attempts at legislative changes which affect its competitive position; for multinational organizations, the current and projected attitudes of the host government and key people; political issues of current or developing interest, which may influence customer demand, competitive position, or the social setting in which the organization does business.

8. *The Physical Environment* — Changes in the physical locale in which the organization conducts its operations; direct ecological effects of those operations on the physical surroundings; possible influences on the efficiency of operations caused by changes in the local environment; changes in human activities which may affect the organization's dealings with its customers, such as automobile traffic, living conditions, travel requirements for the employees, air pollution, physical aspects of procuring materials and shipping goods, etc.; changes in the physical environment which might necessitate a multilocation arrangement of operations, with attendant communication problems and requirements for management control.

These environmental factors are, of course, only suggestions for top-management attention. Top managers of a particular organization will find many more which pertain to their own environments and which would probably not arise from a simple discussion of general environments such as the foregoing. Figure 7-3 illustrates the effects of these environments on the organization.

A few examples may serve to clarify the impact of changes in these various areas on the environmental match. With respect to the Economic Environment, for example, manufacturers of durable consumer goods such as refrigerators and washing machines realize that consumers begin to save money in a downturn, and buy less of their goods. They emphasize lower-price models and push sales more strongly. They also realize that latent buying power built up during the downturn will result in increased sales as the economy improves. They begin to build up inventories to

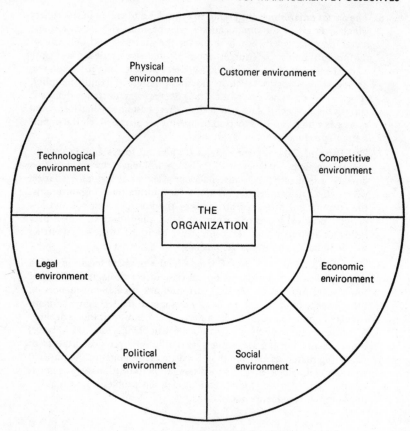

Figure 7–3
The Organization Interacts with a Variety of Environments

prepare for the increased demand caused by consumers replacing their overaged appliances.

The magazine-publishing industry offers another interesting example of adaptation of changes in the Customer Environment. Many mass-circulation magazines went out of business because their executives failed to differentiate between their customers—large advertisers who supplied the bulk of their income—and their readers. As television began to attract the mass-advertising dollar in the early fifties, some publishing executives diversified their operations, abandoned mass-circulation magazines, and developed periodicals focused on well-defined segments of the reading public. But others tried to ride out the storm. The famous *Saturday Evening Post, Life, Look,* and *Collier's* all went under. They went out of business in the face of *increasing* numbers of readers but a decreasing ratio of subscription revenue to circulation cost.

The railroad industry provides an obvious example of failure to adapt to changes in the Competitive Environment. In the 1920s, American railroad companies were some of the strongest and wealthiest enterprises in the world. None of the top-management groups in the industry perceived clearly enough the coming age of the automobile. Nor did they make any major changes in their strategies as long-haul trucking became a reality, and as the airplane came into its own as a passenger and cargo transport-system. Stuck with ancient capital equipment, manual methods for scheduling and marshalling, rolling stock which was largely old and unsafe, and miles of substandard and speed-limited track, American railroads almost perished between the 1950s and 1960s. Airline executives, conversely, saw the enormous increase in business travel, both cross-country and along certain intermetropolitan corridors, and helped it along with convenient schedules, food service, and status features like in-flight movies and private travellers' clubs. Airline companies virtually clinched their superiority over railroads by boldly applying computer technology to flight scheduling and ticket sales, and staging successive upgrades of aircraft as major manufacturers introduced them.

One of the outstanding examples in this century of a change in the Technological Environment was the miniature electronic calculator, made possible by the development of cheap digital microcircuits. Several Japanese firms acted quickly enough to capture a respectable share of the American market, while American firms were "waiting for the price to come down." When the price came down, it dropped with a crash and the Japanese firms were ready. Within less than five years, the electronic calculator virtually pushed the conventional electromechanical models right out of the market. Electronics manufacturers had to rush their product decisions to stay abreast of this wildly changing Environment.

The office photocopier—commonly referred to as the "Xerox machine," proving the advertising value of arriving first with a catchy name—offers an excellent example of a change which brought important impacts in the Legal Environment. Books, magazines, printed sheet music, and other visual media which publishers could previously protect from distribution by others now find their way into mass circulation by way of the office copier. Copyright laws still govern, but they are virtually unenforceable. Before the copier, only those with the means to republish the article of interest—and presumably interest in making a profit from doing so— offered any competition to the copyright owner. Now, virtually anyone can make a clean, useful copy of a copyrighted article for a few cents. University Associates, a San Diego publisher of specialty books for the behavioral sciences, adopted a stated policy of *encouraging* limited copying of its materials by trainers for use in seminars. They attempt to protect copying rights only for large-scale distribution at a profit.

The Social Environment has changed enormously over the past ten to twenty years, and we can find many examples of organizations which have—and have not—adapted well. American military organizations, particularly the Army and Marine Corps, have been devastated by the effects of broad social changes leading to a wholesale challenge of the traditional role of the soldier as an obedient functionary with no right to assert his individuality or personal needs. Old-line officers and non-commissioned officers suffer from "future shock"—to use Alvin Toffler's now-famous term—as their pre-war value systems undergo the enormous pressure of a changing social pattern.

Pornography offers another interesting example of social change. *Playboy* magazine rocketed to the status of one of the most profitable publishing ventures of all time, during a period when American sexual values underwent an enormous transition. Television, movies, rock music, and a sophisticated magazine industry helped to create an environment in which Hugh Hefner was able to build a giant publishing empire by selling fantasy experience (packaged with a heavy status appeal) to American males.

Changes in the Political Environment in several Latin American countries during the 1960s placed very severe pressures on some American corporations operating there. Several companies invested large sums to set up oil refineries and manufacturing plants, only to have them seized and nationalized by revolutionary governments.

Complex aspects of the Physical Environment came into play when construction of the 800-mile trans-Alaska oil pipeline ran into one snag after another as contractors discovered how much they didn't know about the Alaskan tundra and its ecology. Construction operations, as well as the presence of the pipeline itself, caused substantial alterations to the local terrain and the associated animal life. Conservation officials blocked the headlong rush of the pipeline contractors, and forced them to implement proper erosion-control methods, to elevate many sections of pipe so as not to disturb migration routes used by moose, caribou, and other animals, and to control siltation by bridging rivers and streams instead of using culverts.

Ideally, this process of studying the organization's environment would proceed on a continuous basis, perhaps with formal examination of the findings at periodic intervals. A good example of careful attention to the environment would be a system of quarterly strategy meetings, during which the top management team hears formal briefings on the status of the organization and its various environmants, supplemented by occasional discussions and informal reviews. The chief executive officer can do much to foster this habit of studying the environment simply by making it a frequent topic of conversation in executive meetings. Top managers themselves may provide the best sources of insight into environmental processes.

As the top managers develop a clearer understanding of the organization's own peculiar environmental match, and of the ongoing changes in the environment around them, they naturally develop opinions and preferences about what the environmental match should become. This third step is the all-important process of plotting strategy and setting objectives.

Choosing the "Next Move"

With the leadership of the chief executive officer, the members of the team spell out the nature of the course changes—if any—they must make to keep the organization effectively matched to its changing environment. They may decide that things are going very well and choose to make no significant changes to the organization. Or, they may decide to anticipate a major environmental change by starting an organizational change process well in advance. In either case, top management gives steering signals to the rest of the people in the organization, based on a thorough and thoughtful study of the environment and the problems and opportunities confronting the organization. And clearly stated objectives represent the desired-result conditions which they can point to in helping the employees of the organization to understand what they must do. This matter of strategic thrust deserves considerable top-management attention. The organization's chief executive and the top-action people must be able to state, in simple and operational terms, what the organization's "next move" is. This clear and simple strategy statement provides the organizing concept which makes sense of the objectives-setting process. It gives the big picture to all levels of the organization.

Some examples may help to clarify the creative aspects of this thinking process. Theodore Vail, for instance, went down in management history as chief executive officer of American Telephone and Telegraph when he said, "Our business is service." Although deceptively simple, this choice of words in 1910 opened the way for expansion to a truly nationwide operation. It enabled the Bell System to grow into a gigantic privately owned monopoly and to circumvent government attempts at nationalization by building a strong foundation of customer satisfaction. Vail and his top-management team evolved a strategy of actually *encouraging* government regulation in order to soften any tendencies toward government ownerhsip or control. Incidentally, Vail did not have an easy time of selling the other executives on this strategic thrust. In fact, the conservative bankers once forced him out of his job. Not until ten years later did the floundering executive group invite him to return and do what had to be done.

The Sears story offers another example of a wise strategic thrust. Sears, Roebuck and Company became the largest retail company in the world, and one of the most profitable businesses ever, by getting goods to its customers. At the turn of the century, Sears management decided to focus on the farmer as its prime customer. They recognized immediately that they would have to develop an effective distribution channel, since farmers were spread all over the country and were relatively immobile. They settled on the mail-order approach, and opened up an enormous economic trend which lasted for many years. Retail stores in cities offered a reliable source of business as well, but the fact that farmers made up over 80 percent of the general population meant that their individual small purchases would add up to an enormous buying power. And in the mid-twenties, as the automobile made farmers more mobile, as they migrated rapidly to the cities to take industrial jobs, and as the American middle class emerged with its new buying patterns, Sears management decided on a new thrust. They elected to shift the entire Sears operation into retail sales stores. This meant another sweeping metamorphosis in the entire structure and operation of the company. The fact that farmers now make up less than 10 percent of the American population and Sears has a very healthy retail chain seems to validate these two historical redefinitions of strategic thrust.

IBM offers yet another interesting story in the area of strategic thrust. In the 1940s and early 1950s IBM enjoyed a strong position in what

Thomas Watson called the data-processing industry. With basic patents on punched cards, the company had operated well in this small market. With the coming of the first-generation electronic computers in the early 1950s, IBM executives decided to embark on a major new thrust. This meant moving aggressively into this high-technology market and preparing to become a very large corporation. They correctly predicted both the phenomenal growth of the electronic data-processing industry and that it would center on the business corporation as the prime customer. Incidentally, they did not achieve this new thrust without internal agony. After a series of palace fights, Watson himself was forced out of the chief executive's job and replaced by men with an understanding of the new technology and with risk-taking attitudes.

A variety of strategic failures also offer food for thought. Many organizations have failed to arrive at an operational statement of their "next move," and have floundered about, trying to find the handle. The Catholic Church, for example, as well as many other Christian organizations, has utterly failed to define its "products" or to identify a viable strategic thrust. Whereas the local church in the early part of the century provided a form of social contact in rural communities, people in the modern "mobicentric" society find this contact quite readily in their jobs, social groups, and dense neighborhoods. Churches have failed to maintain their match with this changing customer environment.

The "womens' movement" of the 1970s also floundered about for years without a clear sense of direction. Many active women wasted valuable time and energy, letting off steam on social noisemaking and revenge tactics instead of focussing on worthwhile economic results. Indeed, many historical attempts at grand schemes fell apart because their proponents had not articulated their strategies in operational terms. The "chicken in every pot," the "war to end all wars," and the "war on poverty" all went the same way. Even the American space program languished after the six Apollo landings on the moon, because they had achieved John Kennedy's much publicized objective of "landing a man on the moon and bringing him safely back to Earth, within this decade." NASA had great difficulty making its "next move" sufficiently palatable to the American public and the Congress. With respect to this strategic definition, Peter F. Drucker observes:

> Nothing may seem simpler or more obvious than to know what a company's business is. A steel mill makes steel, a railroad runs trains to carry freight and passengers, an insurance company underwrites fire risks, a bank

lends money. Actually, "What is our business?" is almost always a difficult question and the right answer is usually anything but obvious. . . . That business purpose and business mission are so rarely given adequate thought is perhaps the most important single cause of business frustration and business failure.[7]

Key Result Areas

The single most important rule to remember in deciding on the organization's strategic thrust—its next move—is to *concentrate the resources and energies of the organization on a few Key Result Areas of high value.* We could liken the problem of managing a large organization to that of leading a field army in an attack on another army. A large crowd of people operating in a condition of high activity and at least moderate confusion needs a few very simple instructions. The more complicated the statement of their immediate mission, the more chances they have to become confused and disoriented. The more complex the statement, the more opportunities arise for various individuals to supply their own creative interpretations, thereby diffusing the energies which they should concentrate to achieve the best advantage. By selecting a handful of really important categories for energetic management action—and continuous attention—we can maintain the simplicity of mission and sense of concentration we need. This means we must boil down the results of our environmental analysis and our evaluation of the organization's performance to those key issues essential to survival and growth. It doesn't mean that we wilfully neglect other areas of possible payoff, but rather that we work on them only after we have done all we reasonably can to capitalize on the high-priority areas.

Drucker suggests the following as Key Result Areas for the typical corporation:[8]

1. Marketing
2. Innovation
3. Human Organization
4. Financial Resources
5. Physical Resources
6. Productivity
7. Social Responsibility
8. Profit Requirements

---

[7]Drucker, *Management: Tasks, Responsibilities, Practices,* p. 77.
[8]Drucker, *Management: Tasks, Responsibilities, Practices,* p. 100.

Nonprofit organizations such as government agencies, research foundations, churches, professional societies, and hospitals might have certain other Key Result Areas peculiar to their own operations. These might include areas such as community services, fund-raising requirements, community relations, member service-standards, or patient care.

In any case, the top managers of an organization of any kind need to zero in on a relatively small number of payoff areas and set a few major objectives for each. They should even rank these few Key Result Areas in order of priority to ensure the proper concentration of resources. In implementing these major objectives down through the organization, managers at various levels can subdivide them or break them down into intermediate objectives. This process, however, *is for the most part none of top management's business.* Top managers should concern themselves with top management and grant sufficient latitude to their subordinate managers to achieve the objectives as they see fit. This will get better results and will also help prevent the organization from becoming a paper mill.

This process of concentrating attention requires a surprising level of discipline for top managers. It requires a realistic point of view about their own capabilities to direct and guide the many activities of the organization's people. It means "not letting the reach exceed the grasp." The Italian economist Vilfredo Pareto advanced the point of view which has come to be termed the "80/20 rule." Pareto contended that differences in the likely payoffs resulting from managerial actions did not justify equal attention to all possibilities. He claimed that, typically, 80 percent of the possible payoffs arise from *dealing effectively* with only about 20 percent of the problems and opportunities which arise. Conversely, 20 percent of the problems could possibly consume 80 percent of the manager's time and produce only 20 percent of the possible results. Others have extended the 80/20 rule to other aspects of managing, such as contending that 20 percent of the organization's people get 80 percent of the work done, and so on. For the purposes of setting major objectives, this 80/20 rule offers some useful guidance.

Another convenient term for this process of narrowing down the opportunities to the high-payoff items is "ABC analysis," a term coined by H. Ford Dickie,[9] who used it to focus attention on high-cost items in inventory control. Dickie advocated identifying the "Type-A" items in a situation and focusing attention on them. Items B and C received

[9]H. Ford Dickie, "Hard-Nosed Inventory Management," in Donald G. Hall, ed., *The Manufacturing Man and His Job* (New York: American Management Association, 1966), pp. 238-54.

treatment commensurate with their lower importance in terms of cost and payoff. Alan Lakein applies this same idea in his system of time management.[10] Lakein identifies Type-A items as those requiring high-priority attention *and* offering high payoff. Items in the B Category get taken care of after items in Category A. Category-C items get taken care of after items in Category B. Top managers can use this ABC analysis as they consider the wide variety of strategic issues facing them. By focusing on Type-A issues, they can achieve and maintain the sense of strategic concentration they need in order to do a few things very well, rather than many things poorly. Figure 7-4 illustrates this Key Result Area concept, with emphasis on Type-A items for objective setting.

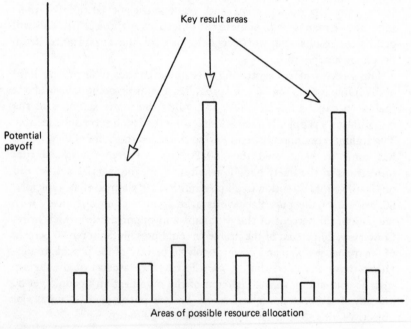

Figure 7-4

Concentrate Resources on a Few Key Result Areas of High Payoff

[10]Alan Lakein, *How to Get Control of Your Time and Your Life* (New York: Signet, 1973).

Special Problems of
Nonprofit Organizations

Throughout this book, we have been proceeding on the premise that managers in nonprofit organizations can manage by objectives just as effectively as their profit-oriented colleagues. The same concepts of payoff orientation and objectives-oriented problem solving apply in the management of any human enterprise. But we must acknowledge that top managers of nonprofit organizations face a more demanding task in charting their course. The same reasons which make it more difficult also make it more imperative for them. Let's explore the key differences between profit-making organizations (PMO's) and nonprofit organizations (NPO's).

The principal difference between the PMO and the NPO lies in their relationships with their customer/client environments. Let's use the term "client" for both types of organizations to emphasize the notion of someone benefitting from the goods or services provided by the organization. For the PMO, which is typically an industrial company, the client supplies the organization's principal form of revenue. The PMO deals with its client by *quid pro quo* — it delivers goods or services for which the client pays directly. The price depends on specific features of the transaction, such as how much of the product, its level of quality, its scarcity, and other conventional supply-and-demand variables. But the NPO leads a somewhat schizophrenic life. It provides goods and services to the client, but it usually receives its principal revenue from another source. There is usually no *quid pro quo* in this situation. Whereas the PMO deals with one environmental entity — the buyer of its output — the NPO deals with two. It must satisfy its clients and its benefactors. They are seldom the same. For example, a county government agency, such as a welfare department, provides services to people who have no money. It gets its operating capital from the county tax base provided by the contributions of those who can afford to live at a level which requires them to pay taxes. A nonprofit cancer-research foundation performs services for the good of the society. But "society" does not donate money to support its operations — wealthy philanthropists and foundations do.

Many NPO's live, to some extent, in both worlds. The typical private college, for example, defrays part of its costs with student tuition fees, but depends heavily on the original endowment and donations from private sources. The typical community church combines fund-raising bake sales and other activities with solicitations for private donations in order to keep going. It also depends heavily on volunteer labor in many of its activities. Some NPO's operate essentially like corporations, managing themselves to a "zero-profit" level.

This key difference between the PMO and the NPO leads to radically different forms of adjustment to their environments and to different kinds of consequences with regard to the performance question. In the profit-making world of commerce, a sort of Darwinian process of "natural selection" operates relentlessly and ruthlessly. The industrial company which does not provide a product or service which its clients want and will pay for simply doesn't survive. It goes under and ceases to exist as an economic enterprise. At any one moment, many industrial firms are going out of business—although many of their managers may not know it. They are progressively losing the quality of their environmental match. Their clients are going elsewhere. We can think of this supply-and-demand process as forming an interaction loop between company and client. Goods and services flow one way and money flows the other.

But for the county agency, for example, the "client" is split into two separate and very different entities. The agency has a client population and a benefactor. It must come to terms with both of these entities. This three-element loop is much more complex and offers some interesting features for study. Figure 7–5 diagrams this interaction loop for the PMO and the NPO.

These two feedback loops differ primarily in the matter of *slack*. The systems analyst would describe the PMO-customer loop as a "tight" one, i.e., one in which the two entities are closely coupled. What one of them does affects the other very directly, and vice versa. But the NPO-client-benefactor loop would be termed a very "loose" loop because of the tenuous nature of the influence exerted by the client on the benefactor.

We would all like to believe that the funding received by the county sheriff's organization depends on the quality of the service which that unit provides to the tax-paying public, and that the public determines through the voting process how the sheriff's department should operate. In principle this is true, but in experience it is not. The time lag of the

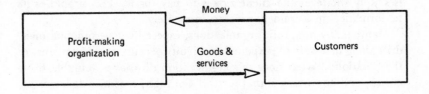

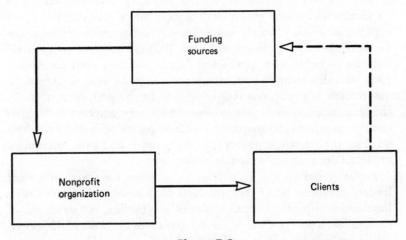

Figure 7–5
The Nonprofit Organization Relates to Its Environment Differently From
the Profit-making Organization

political selection process, coupled with the enormous diversity of performance issues means that the quality of service exerts only a very general
influence on the department's budget. The other important difference
between the PMO and the NPO is that it is usually much more difficult
to specify the NPO's "performance" in terms of dollar value. We usually
have no trouble specifying its costs, but value presents an enormous
problem. What is it worth to a county citizen to have the assurance of
a reasonable state of law and order? What is fire protection worth? What
are public roads worth? By contrast, the value of the PMO's product

is simply whatever the client agrees to pay for it. This simplifies its performance-measurement problem immensely.

Many, many nonprofit organizations, especially governmental ones, drift along in a state of perpetual ambiguity because no one can answer the question: "What does this organization do that is valuable to its clients, and how much is that worth?" For many a county department, state bureau, or federal agency, we simply have a very poor idea of what its operation is worth. Governmental funding processes are mostly *activity-oriented*, i.e., the people who control and allocate the taxpayers' money can specify clearly what activities they are buying, but they usually have little idea what social benefits they are buying. This points to the most important reason why government leaders rarely abolish government organizations—they simply don't know whether most organizations are worth keeping, so they keep them. Political leaders frequently re-organize to redistribute power and funds, and they even create new agencies which compete with others, for these same reasons. And since government organizations mostly operate in the activity-trap mode, they can continue from year to year. This is why government budgets continue to expand and government staffs keep growing in size. Abolishing an obsolete government agency is an active move, and most government organizations are merely *reactive* in their operation.

Public school systems have floundered about for years, with their leaders unable to define their products or to assess their value. Critics have attacked public education variously as too lax, too strict, out of date, too far ahead of the times, and irrelevant to the needs of the society. Educators, administrators, and political leaders still can't seem to agree on what they mean by "a good education." Curriculum development offers a very attractive opportunity for objectives-oriented thinking and design.

All of this means that the managers of the nonprofit organization must think in terms of payoffs and objectives even more than their profit-making colleagues. They must ask the same question: "What is our Business?" and they must wrestle with it continually until they find meaningful, operational answers. These answers must provide the basis for evaluating the contributions which their organizations make to their clients, and for selling their programs to those who provide funds.

In government, this means that those in positions of control and fund allocation—city mayors, county supervisors, state governors and legislators, Congress people and the President—must tighten the accountability loop represented by Figure 7-5. The individual organizational unit leaders usually cannot do this. Top leaders must assess the contributions of these organizations to the community and must demand that they become accountable—both to the client population and to the administration.

Any nonprofit organization needs a well-defined environmental match. Its top managers must evaluate its performance by identifying its principal service categories and setting realistic measures of effectiveness. Then they can apply the management-by-objectives thinking and planning process to decide on organizational strategy.

Many nonprofit executives have had success with the so-called *program-oriented budget* approach to planning and resource allocation. This objectives-oriented approach involves specifying the organization's operation in a number of result-oriented *program areas,* focusing on objectives and measures of performance rather than on activity. Then they establish objectives for each of these Key Result Areas, and estimate resource requirements for achieving them. A companion concept *zero-base budgeting* involves building up the annual departmental budget from an assumed zero level of resources, requiring that each major budget item answer to an agreed objective or measurable achievement. From this discussion, we can see that, not only can nonprofit managers indeed manage by objectives, but *they must* if they ever hope to escape from the Activity-Trap mode which their strange dichotomous relationship with client and benefactor tends to impose on them. The organizational objectives of these managers become their very reason for existence, and if they secure their funds by promising to meet the objectives, then they automatically have a means for assessing their performance.

Letting Go of the Past

An important part of moving into the future is letting go of the past. This means consciously abandoning those programs, products, or services which no longer make sense. Many executives find it extremely difficult to accept the idea that a favorite project simply hasn't produced worthwhile results and probably never will. They find it even more difficult to recognize that a once-healthy product line has turned moribund and no longer attracts the support of the customer. Many an executive who has risen to power on the back of an exciting new "boom" product slides into oblivion clinging to its desiccated carcass. And many a rising executive has unseated an incumbent by ushering in the product which brought with it the new wave of profitability.

In deciding on the organization's next move, its executives must ask not only "What new strategic thrust shall we undertake?" but also "What product, service, or program must we get rid of, to free us for the future?" They must recognize that the product which made such a beautiful environmental match ten years ago may have started dragging the organization down toward disaster. Yesterday's asset may have become tomorrow's liability if the environmental conditions which made it such a sensible move have ceased to exist.

Top managers should review *all* major aspects of their organization as they reflect on the matter of strategy. For each of their major products, services, or programs, they should ask themselves, "Knowing what we now know, do we consider this a good investment of our resources? If someone proposed it as a brand new venture today, would we choose to embark upon it?" If the answer comes out "no," then they had better seriously consider abandoning the enterprise. If the answer is "yes," then they have revalidated that line of endeavor as part of their consciously established strategy for the next planning period.

Strategic Planning

Once the organization's top managers have confirmed their idea of the direction in which they must steer the organization, they must next make a strategic plan. This step will proceed smoothly if they have accomplished the preceding steps well. If they haven't, then strategic planning will offer more agony than assurance.

We could say that the stated objectives and the desired new environmental match provide the "want to do." Strategic planning provides the "how to do." Let's review the basic principles of strategic long-range planning.

1. Get the entire top-management team constructively involved in the planning process.
2. Allow plenty of freedom for controversy, creative thinking, and constructive debate; make use of seminar-style executive sessions
3. Question the organization's basic philosophies from time to time; make planning a continuing process rather than an annual event.

4. Support the thinking and planning process with comprehensive studies, planning data, and management analyses if they are needed.

5. Do not delegate the planning *process* to a "planner"; have one executive put together the plan, but only after all members of the team have contributed their ideas and opinions.

6. Have a written plan which is simple, fairly brief, and specific; make it available throughout the organization to those who need to understand it and work to meet its goals.

7. Focus the plan on just a few key result areas of high payoff; do not dissipate energy and resources with a multitude of objectives which obscure the real winners.

8. Gain commitment for the plan throughout the organization by including the key action people in the planning process to whatever extent is feasible.

9. Make the plan reasonable; focus on realistic achievement.

10. Build into the plan an automatic process for reviewing it from time to time, for changing it as necessary, and even for abandoning major portions of it if unforeseen circumstances require it.

Getting down to Work

Probably the single most important rule in making and using strategic plans is: *work the plan.* The members of the top-management team must establish the plan with full intention of beginning immediately to do the things they have decided on. The plan must not be just a stack of paper, full of abstractions and generalities. It must be a prescription for top-management action. It must set forth those few key objectives they want to attain, and it must specify the actions they will take in order to mobilize the resources of the organization to attain them.

One effective way to maintain a high level of executive thrust in carrying out the plan is to appoint individual executives as "quarterbacks" for selected objectives. Since the best plan is usually one with no more than three or four basic objectives, this means that any individual executive can focus his attention strongly on his assigned mission and tend to it continually in the course of his routine duties. Whenever possible, the responsibility for accomplishing an objective should rest with the executive whose functional responsibility closely parallels the nature of the objective. In this way, the chief executive officer can focus the strengths of his top managers rather than diffuse the objective across the whole staff. He can look to one individual in each case for results, and that individual can call upon the others as necessary for the support he needs in achieving the objective. This approach provides a natural means for merging the objectives-oriented "change in course" with the ongoing day-to-day operations of the organization. The executive who has responsibility for a particular objective can draw the attention of the organization toward that need, without disrupting their routine business any more than necessary.

This approach has another advantage, in that it tends to ensure a continuity of attention to the objectives down through the organization. When the objective has an individual quarterback, then the activities required to achieve it are shaped by person-to-person contact rather than by the more abstract process of "organizational" communication. The executive can explain the nature of the objective to the subordinates and guide them in achieving it during the course of their ongoing work.

8

Operational
Management by
Objectives

The job of the "operational" manager—i.e., the head of an organizational subunit—differs from that of the top manager only in degree. The operational manager must do virtually everything the top manager does for his own unit, but the relative emphasis differs. Whereas the top manager is highly concerned with the basic direction of the entire organization, the unit manager is concerned with the basic direction of his own group within the framework of the larger organization. Both must concern themselves with the match between their respective organizations and their environments, both must set objectives, both must plan for their accomplishment, and both must evaluate results and give day-to-day guidance to their employees.

Any manager, at any level, in any kind of an organization, can adopt the behavior pattern we call management by objectives. In this chapter, we will examine the methods and techniques which the operational manager can use in managing by objectives. These techniques, together with the objectives-oriented behavior pattern described in Chapter 3 and the skills of analyzing problems and setting objectives described in Chapter 6, form the foundation for high-performance management.

The Management Cycle

One of the many simple ways to categorize and describe managerial behavior is with the notion of the "management cycle," which consists of three overlapping functions:

1. *Direction* — Giving guidance to the workers; stating objectives, assigning tasks, delegating problems, giving direct instructions, and helping them to understand what constitutes good performance
2. *Visibility* — observing ongoing processes and studying key measures of performance
3. *Control* — Comparing the observed results with the expected or desired results, and giving new direction as required

Figure 8-1 illustrates this process. As a unit manager goes about his day's work, he generally deals with ongoing work processes and the problems which arise in connection with those processes. He discusses a task with an employee who has hit a snag in carrying it out. He confers with several employees together to help them clarify their individual roles in an ongoing project. He discovers that one of the employees is confused about the procedure for a certain task, and he explains it. He spots an emerging problem area and assigns one of the employees to study it and recommend a solution. He decides to improve a certain aspect of the unit's capability, and he calls a conference to discuss possible courses of action. From time to time, he gives direct instructions to individuals concerning isolated situations which require action.

Objectives as Tools
for Managing

What part do objectives play in this day-to-day process of managing an organizational unit? What part does objectives-oriented behavior play on the part of the manager as well as on the part of the employees? We can answer these two essential questions by dealing with an objective as 1) a thinking aid and 2) a communications tool.

First, the manager can employ the MBO problem-solving process defined in Chapter 6. Proceeding from a generalized want, which he may only be able to express as a fuzzy, the manager can become progres-

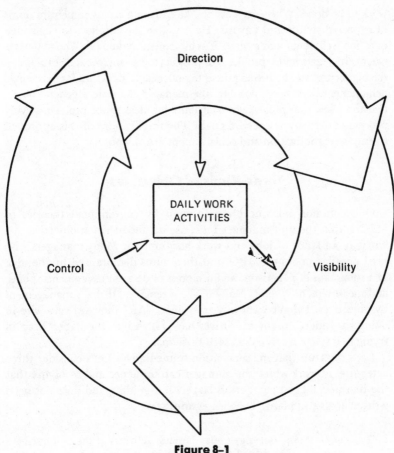

Figure 8–1
The Management Cycle

sively more specific until he arrives at a goal which is specific, performance-oriented, intrinsically rewarding for the person who must achieve it, realistic, and observable. He can then use this goal as an aiming point as he shapes and guides the activities of his workers day by day. If the manager has studied his organization and its environment carefully, this goal will be one of a few high-payoff items in his managerial portfolio. It will be part of a simple and self-consistent system of goals which he uses as a basis for managing the unit. Second, the manager can use objectives as tools for communicating with the employees about the work to be done. Whenever possible, he can state an assignment in terms of expected results and payoffs. He can give the employee a clear idea of a "job well done" and a sense of achievement in doing it. The managers can also delegate entire problems or projects to his employees by explaining the big picture and by helping them to understand his desires for long-range achievement. Whenever possible, the manager can state a general objective and allow the employee to contribute his ideas to the problem-solving process of arriving at specific goals. The implications of this approach to employee motivation and commitment are obvious.

Three Kinds of Objectives

One common misconception fostered by conventional theories of MBO is that the unit manager must use detailed written objectives for virtually all kinds of jobs and work assignments. Many managers who read popular books on MBO find themselves demoralized by the idea of a mountain of paperwork and a morass of detailed assignments, plans, and measurement systems. Many of them remark, "If that's management by objectives, I don't want any part of it." And they are very wise in doing so. Indeed, many executives have fallen into the Paper Trap in trying to implement so-called MBO systems.

Let's clear up that misconception immediately. Let's consider three categories of work which the manager can influence and recognize that the first and biggest category is largely self-guiding and does not need written goals and plans. These categories are:

1. *Routine Work* — The day-to-day business activities of the unit; well-understood tasks assigned to individuals for completion; routine duties of a repeatable nature; working-level problems which arise and which the employees know how to handle; things needing attention which the employees can tend to on their own initiative; relatively minor difficulties requiring the manager's occasional advice, guidance, or decisions.

2. *Problems* — Significant unanticipated events or situations which require that the manager and one or more employees cooperate to decide what to do; unusual changes in work load; unexpected snags in carrying out a major task or project; a change in policy by upper management; discovery of an impending condition of significance to the group's performance or the well-being of its members.

3. *Opportunities* — Possibilities for improving the performance of the unit by taking initiative in anticipation of upcoming events; perceived

changes or trends in the organization's environment which offer a chance
to enhance its environmental match; actions which the manager or his
employees can take to bring about desirable environmental changes.

Let us agree right now that the second and third categories of work
call for aggressive objectives-oriented management behavior. For these
two types of challenge, management by objectives applies very well.
For the first category of work, it does not. Yet unfortunately, many
organizational approaches to MBO focus on the routine activities—
those least in need of managerial guidance and creative thinking. This
is the basis for the "MBO Rat-Race" treated more thoroughly in Chapter 10.

This is not to say that the manager need not communicate with the
employees on routine work processes. It simply means that he does not
squander his energy—or theirs—on relatively formal plans, programs,
and reporting schemes for activities which they know how to do well,
and which he believes they will do well.

Certainly, an effective manager will assign routine duties clearly and
distinctly and will establish standards of performance for them. This
is merely good supervisory practice. The manager who has not done
this is not yet ready to manage by objectives. And mistaking this process
for management by objectives will inevitably lead to a Paper Mill instead
of a lively, results-oriented group atmosphere.

Figure 8-2 portrays the balance among these three kinds of work
from the manager's point of view. It also shows the typical kinds of direction the manager provides in each case. The relative proportions of
Routine Work, Problem Situations, and Opportunity Situations will
vary from one organizational unit to another. Controlling factors here
include the nature of the unit's mission, the intensity of the work load,
the levels of competence and attitudes of the employees, the unit's relations
with other units, and the manager's style and methods.

Perhaps this simple view of the daily work will help to dispel the mythol-
ogy about how to apply management by objectives as a technique. The
Routine Activities will settle into a kind of equilibrium condition, such
as that described in Chapter 7. This is as it should be. The manager
should only disturb the equilibrium of Routine Work when he finds
it necessary to change it as a result of Problems or Opportunities. He
should maintain a Routine system of visibility and guidance, without
undue attention to paper work and detail.

This attitude toward the work load actually frees the manager and
the employees to focus their energies to best advantage. By keeping the

Figure 8–2
Three Categories of Work Activity

Routine Work of the unit underway, without necessary paper work, they can focus their creative energies on solving Problems and capitalizing on Opportunities. They can use the skills of analyzing problems and setting objectives, discussed in Chapter 6, and the strategy of focusing on Key Result Areas, as a means for improving the unit's performance. In this way, the manager and the employees think and act as a team, with everyone having a part to play in shaping the daily activities.

Setting Priorities and
Managing Time

Every manager needs a sense of the "big picture" with respect to the unit's operation. This involves the feeling that the manager grasps the essentials of the management job, understands the day-to-day activities of the unit, and can separate the really important problems and issues from the unimportant. This calls for a highly developed sense of priority. Indeed, one of the most critical managerial skills is the ability to focus on what really counts and to tend to it first.

The manager who lacks this strategic skill of focusing energy is usually on a treadmill to some extent. Such a manager is usually oversupplied with matters which demand his attention and undersupplied with time to think about the organization and where it is going. The manager and the organization operate perpetually in the "crunch mode." "Fire fighting" and crisis operation become the organizational norm.

Symptoms of crunch-mode management are easy to recognize:

- The manager is usually overworked; he comes in early, leaves late, or takes work home on a routine basis.
- The manager imposes impossible schedules as a matter of routine.
- There are many "surprises"—unanticipated problems or demands on his time and the time of the employees.
- Departmental morale is on the wane; complaining, cynical attitudes and lack of enthusiasm are common among employees.
- In-fighting is on the increase; the members of the organization vent their anger and frustration upon each other.
- Neither the manager nor the employees can state, in simple terms, what they are trying to accomplish.

The presence of the crunch mode does not necessarily mean that the manager or his employees are incompetent. It simply means that they are misoriented. Because of their preoccupation with the present situation, they cannot answer the question, "Why are we doing what we're doing?" They lack a clear sense of direction. They focus on *doing,* not on *going.*

The objectives-oriented manager, on the other hand, manages a "results" department. The manager and the employees produce results which have significant value because they have separated the important from the unimportant. They operate with a strategic sesne of payoff.

The skill of *time management* enables the manager to develop and maintain this strategic sense. Time management is a habit pattern characterized by:

1. Making a written list of the "things to do"—activities required of the manager, either in response to upcoming problems and demands, or by the manager's own initiative
2. Arranging the things to do in order of priority as determined by the expected payoff of each item
3. Doing the things on the list in priority order to the greatest reasonable extent
4. Adding items to the list as they arise and crossing off others as they are completed

Time management requires that the manager maintain an organized, written list, and use the list as a guide for *doing first things first*. Alan Lakein,[1] a specialist in time management techniques, suggests that a manager rank the things to do in three categories:

1. "Must-do" items
2. "Should-do" items
3. "Might-do" items

Lakein further suggests that the manager grant first-priority status to only a few items, with a larger number assigned to the second category, and a still larger number assigned to third priority. This ensures that the priority system will not defeat its own purpose by offering an unreasonable number of number-one items.

A manager skilled in time management will frequently review the list of things to do and will find ways to combine items or to accomplish two or more of them at the same time. Such a manager will also question every single item as it arises, to decide whether it really needs doing and whether it can be delegated to someone else. This amounts to an assertive attitude toward the demands of the work environment. The manager continually makes choices about how to spend valuable time and about how to get the highest payoff for that time.

[1]Alan Lakein, *How to Get Control of Your Time and Your Life* (New York: Signet, 1973).

The notion of *payoff* forms the basis for any attempt to "prioritize" managerial and employee activities. When faced with a time conflict, the manager asks, "Of all the things I could possibly choose to do with my time at this moment, which will bring the best payoff?" The manager includes an item on the list of things to do only if the item has a payoff clearly associated with it. That is, the required action must lead to a result which has a distinct value for the manager as an individual and for the unit as a whole. The effective time manager will scrutinize all "miscellaneous" activities and time wasters and eliminate them if they do not meet some reasonable payoff criteria.

The time-management point of view holds that the manager has only a given number of hours in the day and only a reasonable store of physical and creative energy. By attacking the things to be done in priority order, the manager ensures that, when time or energy runs out (and as other important demands continue to pile up), any neglected items will cause only a minimum loss of opportunity or minimum inconvenience.

Just as the manager analyzes the long-term direction of the unit and sets objectives which capitalize on opportunities, so does he add items to the list of things to do which are *opportunity-oriented*. The list will probably contain both reactive items—i.e., things to do in response to upcoming conditions and problems—and anticipatory items, which will bring payoffs in the future. Some of the reactive items and anticipatory items will bring positive results. Others will merely stave off negative results.

Having learned the time-management discipline, the manager can train the employees of the organization to manage their time effectively as well. In giving assignments, the manager can grant them an appropriate degree of freedom in scheduling the work, so they can arrange their daily activities largely as they see fit.

When one assigned task conflicts with another, the manager and the employee can discuss the conflict and resolve it in favor of the highest overall payoff. Thus, the notions of payoff and priority form a basis for organizational effectiveness.

In a broader sense, the manager keeps the employees' attention focused on key result areas, which offer maximum payoff potential. The objectives-oriented manager recognizes that there are usually more things to be done than time and energy permit and that not all of the possibilities offer equal payoff. In setting the major objectives for the unit, the manager identifies those which offer the highest available payoff and concentrates resources on their achievement.

Management by Objectives
as "Project Management"

Having decided to treat routine work routinely and to deal with problems and opportunities by an objectives-oriented process, we can narrow down the problem of managing by objectives considerably. We can think of a problem to be solved, or an opportunity to be attacked, as a situation requiring a conscious—and preferably minimal—disturbance in the prevailing equilibrium. That is, the manager elects to impose his influence on the ongoing daily activities in such a way as to channel a part of the energy into solutions to problems, or into advances over the status quo. We can consider each of these interventions in the social system as a *"project"*—that is, it has a specific purpose, it influences the employees over a finite period of time, and it has a clearly recognizable result. In this sense, then, management by objectives is merely "project management."

Let's pursue this very important point further. When the manager spots a problem area, he can immediately begin to apply the MBO problem-solving process defined in Chapter 6. He can treat the matter as a special project. He can state his wants, specify the desired end conditions and payoffs, identify possible actions which will solve the problem by bringing about those end conditions, and make a plan of action. This plan tells him how to guide his employees in their activities to solve the problem. The larger the problem, the more comprehensive the problem-solving process must become. At some point, the manager will probably choose to prepare a written plan to help clarify the goals and required actions for the employees. The manager should, however, confine this relatively formal planning approach to those few significant result areas requiring this kind of attention.

Similarly, the manager—and his employees—can attack a recognized opportunity, using the same MBO problem-solving process. A perceived change or trend in the unit's environment enables them to specify the desired goal conditions, to identify possible actions, and to make a plan for achieving them. This becomes an "improvement project" for the unit.

We can picture a unit manager who manages by objectives, and a group of objectives-oriented employees, in something like the following way. Each of the employees has predefined areas of responsibility. Each knows what his primary job functions are, knows how to do them, and knows the standards of performance which the manager and his co-workers expect of him. The employee works more or less independently on these routine tasks, unless he meets with a problem he is unable to handle. He consults the unit manager with the problem, and they jointly work out a solution based on agreed-upon goals. With whatever assistance he needs from the manager or his co-workers, he proceeds to solve the problem, usually working it into his day's schedule of things to be done. Meanwhile, the unit manager has a small portfolio of high-payoff opportunity-type objectives, and he gives directions to his employees such that their day-to-day activities make progress toward these goals. From time to time, he reviews progress with them, and discusses the feasibility of the goals as well as other possibilities for improving the organization's performance.

The typical employee, then, will be doing a day's work based on the combined influence of several factors: his routine duties, actions he takes to solve problems which have appeared, and actions taken to achieve specified unit-level goals. All of the directions for his activities will have come, in one way or another, from day-to-day discussions with the manager.

This point of view enables us to simplify our picture of the requirements for managing by objectives. We can consider it to be something like the superposition of a few key development projects, based on perceived problems and opportunities, on top of the ongoing constructive routine activities which constitute the unit's equilibrium activity.

Decision Making by Objectives

The manager can also use the objectives orientation in dealing with decision issues which arise. Following a procedure something like that given in Chapter 6, the manager can focus on desirable payoffs—the decision objectives—in evaluating the various known courses of action. The objectives orientation helps the manager to balance the need for positive action with the need to make sound decisions which stand the test of time.

Decision-making "speed" forms an important part of every manager's general approach to problem solving. As Figure 8-3 illustrates, individual managers range from overcautious to overhasty in choosing a course of action. This decision-making style tends to be fairly consistent for any one individual. Those who ponder interminably over even the simplest

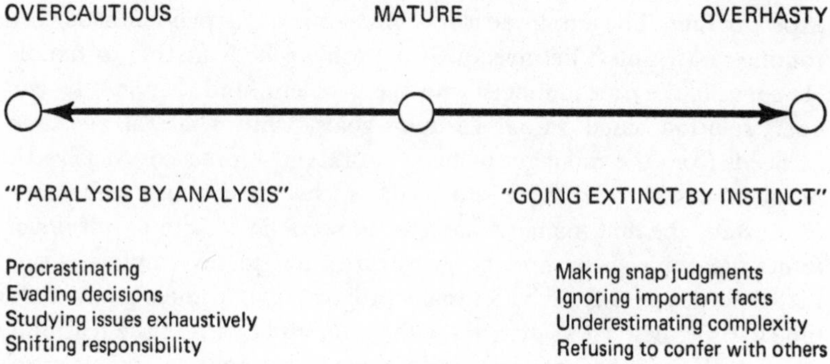

OVERCAUTIOUS   MATURE   OVERHASTY

"PARALYSIS BY ANALYSIS"   "GOING EXTINCT BY INSTINCT"

Procrastinating   Making snap judgments
Evading decisions   Ignoring important facts
Studying issues exhaustively   Underestimating complexity
Shifting responsibility   Refusing to confer with others

Figure 8–3
Managers Vary in Their Decision-making Styles

decisions, who put off decisions, who call for more and more fact finding and analyses, and who foster never-ending debates, seem paralyzed. They generally fear the accountability that comes with deciding. They end up in a state of "paralysis by analysis." Conversely, those who make snap judgements, who offer quick opinions, who always seem to have the solution, and who generally "shoot from the hip," usually end up going "extinct by instinct." These people enjoy the sense of quick action and try to convey an image of being mentally sharp and sure of themselves.

Both of these extremes are equally disastrous. While the procrastinator fumbles with the decision issue, the employees can't proceed effectively; they lose time and use their energies inefficiently. On the other hand, the employees of the hip-shooter must frequently second-guess his poorly through-out decisions, and repair the damage done by previous ones.

The objectives-oriented manager can use the principle of *creative procrastination* in approaching major decision issues. This principle states: *"I will delay actually choosing the final course of action until that point when taking any extra time would jeopardize the quality of the decision; I will delay no longer than that but will make the best decision I can at that point, based on the available knowledge."*

This attitude leads to a strategic approach to major decisions. The manager refuses to be stampeded by pressures for quick action, but also accepts the inevitable risk and uncertainty associated with every decision. Such a manager uses time constructively to anticipate major decisions and to study them in depth so as to clarify the various options and to reduce the associated risks. He realizes that information is the most important resource in decision making and takes time to get the information he needs to decide effectively.

Some Examples of
MBO Applications

Let's consider a few operational applications of management by objectives within a typical medium-sized organization. A typical problem which invites objectives-oriented thinking is "equal employment opportunity." Suppose the head of a medium-sized corporate division decides to improve the opportunities within the unit for women and minority workers to move into management positions. The manager can establish a goal condition of having women and minorities represented in the management ranks according to the same proportions by which they make up the general community from which the company draws its work force. He can then compare these goal figures with the present ratios of the organization and determine what progress is necessary to achieve the desired condition of equal representation. With the help of a qualified consultant or human-resources development expert, the manager can define possible actions. These might include special hiring programs, special training programs, career-development programs, and indoctrination of managers in nondiscriminatory hiring and promotion practices. Typically, an organization will prepare an "affirmative action plan," which spells out the goals and a timetable for achieving them as well as the principal actions to be taken.

Another realistic example of a management-by-objectives problem lies in the area of changing an organization's operation over to the metric system of measurement. The manager of a large engineering department may decide to change the entire operation of the group to the metric standard, or to create a condition of "bilingual" practice, using the metric and the English system of measures interchangeably. He can specify the goal conditions in terms of individual skills in converting measurements from one system to the other, the existence of drawings and specifications with dual units of measurement, and the existence of files and reference handbooks giving engineering and manufacturing data in both systems.

Once the manager has spelled out the conditions he desires, he can identify specific actions he can take to bring them about. He can acquire training aids and working materials which promote the use of metric units; he can conduct training workshops in metric measurement and conversion; and he can appraise individual performance and feed back the results in an encouraging way to the employees. He can consider granting prizes or rewards for demonstrated competence in using the new system. He can then prepare a written plan which spells out the goals and a timetable with required actions for meeting them.

"Turn-around management" offers another very fruitful application of management-by-objectives principles. An industrial company may have a division which has languished for years, failing to achieve the potential which top management believes it has. A typical move would be to appoint an aggressive manager to head the division, with the mission of revitalizing it. The turn-around manager would assess the major dimensions of its performance, such as sales, product design, quality, cost control, and production. He would also pay particular attention to the management strength of the organization itself. The manager would then lay out realistic objectives in each of the key result areas and assign responsibilities to his subordinate managers for meeting them. He would probably also institute an intensive program of management development, possibly with the services of an organization-development consultant. He would develop an emergency "get-well" plan, perhaps for six months' operation. As the organization began to respond to the new direction, the manager could then develop a more routine planning process covering a full year and a general projection for five years or more.

Still another example of a management-by-objectives application is in the management of a large-scale project, of any kind at all. The U.S. Department of Defense employs the objectives-oriented concept of large project management and has developed some very sophisticated techniques for planning and controlling huge efforts. A project manager may elect to build an organization specifically dedicated to one single project of great magnitude, such as the development of a nuclear reactor plant or design and construction of an advanced airplane.

In such a case, the entire organization would be designed around the project at hand. This is not at all unusual for large-scale efforts. The project manager would define clearly the objectives of the project, in terms of specifiable end results and "deliverable" items. For a long-term project, the manager would also establish intermediate objectives as guideposts in managing the effort. He would select certain key points in the course of the project as points for intensive management reveiw and, possibly, decision making. These "milestones," together with the end objectives, would constitute the basic purposes of the project team. He would then confer with the members of the project team and plan out the many actions required, assigning each a completion date and a specific set of criteria for completion. The manager would assemble all of these items into one overall master schedule, which would tell the members of the project team what they must accomplish and what performance criteria the manager will use in evaluating results. Then the project organization would proceed to carry out the plan, measuring results against the stated objectives and feeding back the differences to the project manager for consideration and possible action.

Plans, Programs, and Performance

Every manager has to settle the question, "How much paperwork?" in an individual, personal way. Trying to manage a group solely by word-of-mouth direction and control creates inevitable problems for all but the smaller units doing the most routine kinds of work. Employees can seldom be sure what is expected of them or when they have done their jobs well. A unit with very little written guidance or exchange of written information tends to become a "Fire Department" rather quickly, with the workers and the manager typically responding to whichever problem currently causes them the most anxiety.

Conversely, a manager with a penchant for paper work can create a Paper Mill in short order. Such an organization begins to produce, distribute, and circulate documents as if they constituted its principal product. Frequently, people caught up in a Paper Mill hesitate to try anything new because they dread the huge increase in paper work which it will entail. Too much planning and programming can create as much difficulty and inefficiency as too little.

Written plans and programs within the unit should serve at least three purposes. First, a plan establishes a clear understanding between the manager and the employee of what they must do to achieve the agreed objective. A good plan shows what the employee will do, what part the manager will play in the project, and the time scale for the entire enterprise. It focuses on observable activities and spells out observable measures of achievement which should result from those activities. Second, it helps those within the group communicate more effectively when the program requires their joint efforts. One lead person can usually get the cooperation of other group members by helping them to understand the overall objective, what they need to do to help the effort, and how they will need to interact with one another as the activity progresses. Third, a written plan helps the manager to assess progress toward the unit's selected goals by comparing accomplishments with predictions. The ability to review a few major project plans and assess progress in these areas gives the manager a confident feeling of understanding the big picture of the unit's operation, as well as a feeling of responsive control over the daily operations. This enables the manager to make day-to-day decisions and assignments within the content of an overall framework of long-term performance.

The choice a manager must make concerning the relative degree of formal planning and controlling involves the manager's own style of managing, the diversity and complexity of the unit's work activities, and the work styles of the employees. Specific factors include:

1. The number of employees under the manager's direct supervision
2. The general level of job skills on the part of the employees
3. The proportion of the unit's work which is routine and fully delegated
4. The proportion of nonroutine work requiring minute-to-minute supervision, versus proportion which can be delegated to longer-term accomplishment
5. The complexity of nonroutine work and the need to give general written guidance for long-term performance
6. The number of separate projects or delegated activities which require occasional management review and guidance
7. The manager's memory for details and general inclination to keep objectives and plans in mind from day to day
8. The relative ease of day-to-day communication between manager and employees, and among employees; degree to which unit members work physically close to one another and can discuss the details of a project freely and often

In general, a manager does not need many written plans or formally established work projects when the group is small, when face-to-face communication is easy, when a large proportion of the unit's work is routine, when the nonroutine work is largely simple and straightforward and requires little interaction among group members, and when they are fully competent to do the work. The mangager would do well to consider formal work projcets and written plans, however, when the group is large and functionally diversified, when a large proportion of the work is nonroutine or highly complex, when circumstances make face-to-face communication difficult or impractical, or when the employees need an unusually high level of management guidance in certain phases of the work.

Let's construct a hypothetical picture of a typical work group to see how a manager might establish the general approach to plans and programs within an objectives-oriented pattern of managing. Let's consider a service department within a corporate manufacturing division whose mission is to conduct technical experiments and tests on various kinds of materials which the company might want to use in making its product. The group consists of a manager, a senior scientist, four test engineers, a test aide and a clerk-typist. Its major "clients" are a particular branch within the company's engineering division and two other departments within the manufacturing division itself. The unit's daily work consists of getting samples of new industrial materials, as well as those currently in use within the company, and testing them for properties of interest to the client groups. It also has the responsibility for investigating potential new materials and publishing useful information about their possible applications.

The new manager of the unit finds that it operates quite informally, with virtually no formal systems except the test plans, test procedures, and test reports which the employees prepare for the individual test projects. He finds that the test work occupies most of the unit's attention, with the other department functions receiving little more than a "lick and a promise."

In cooperation with the key employees of the group, the manager assesses the unit's current performance and mode of operation. They answer the question, "What's our business?" with something like, "Our business is providing technical information of recognized value to the A, B, and C groups." This leads to a definition of the operational modes of routine testing, technical consultation preparing internal publications, maintaining a departmental technical-data base, monitoring industrial materials developments, and exploratory testing of new materials of possible interest.

Each of these key result areas has a specified set of accomplishments which the manager and the staff believe to be reasonable. The manager assigns the jobs of monitoring industrial developments and building the technical-data base to the senior scientist, with the instruction to prepare a project plan for achieving the objective. The senior scientist is also instructed to recommend a reasonable budget, in manpower and dollars, for the exploratory test program. In a sense, the manager has appointed the senior scientist a "project manager" in the specific area of responsibility.

The manager subdivides the remaining functional areas similarly, taking care to give each individual a complete area of responsibility whenever possible. They prepare plans to meet the agreed objectives in the various key result areas, and the manager reviews their plans with them. They reconcile the various plans with one another, eliminating duplication and ensuring that they have accounted for all functional objectives. Then the manager develops the departmental budget and a general work plan for the year, getting the advice of the employees as necessary.

At this point, the plans and programs within our hypothetical unit look something like this:

1. A two-page general plan for the department's coming-year operation, written by the manager and available for general reference, gives key result areas and selected objectives for each area.
2. A departmental budget, keyed to the key result areas.
3. A one-page project plan for each of the functional areas; the plan for routine testing will contain a general forecast of client demands to the extent possible.
4. Any other plans the manager may have made as a result of the evaluation and goal-setting process; for example, plans for training staff members, acquiring new equipment, or improving the work facilities.

The manager can choose to simply keep a copy of each of the plans in a file folder or a looseleaf notebook, referring to them from time to time and using them as a basis for day-to-day discussions with the unit employees about progress and performance. Each employee should keep a copy of the plan for his special area of operation and review it occasionally to maintain perspective in the daily work situation.

This unpretentious planning process does not disrupt the day-to-day routine of conducting tests and writing up the results. It merely sets that mainstream process in perspective. The day's work still consists of discussing test work with engineers and production specialists, setting test requirements, writing test plans and procedures, doing the tests, and writing test reports. Insofar as the employees know how to do these things, no interventions by the manager are necessary. If adequate job standards and various technical procedures are available, the manager does not need additional paperwork. This set of simple, streamlined plans should suffice for direction, visibility, and control in such a department.

In this application of management by objectives, note that *everybody plans*. Most of the plans originate with the employees, not with the manager. The employee who thinks through the actions required to achieve an objective tends to "own" the objective and the plan as well. With a light touch of guidance from the manager, the employee can develop a realistic and workable plan which will guide his own actions from day to day. These plans become communication tools within the unit and enable its members to keep their attention focused on results. The employees become "self-managing" to a great extent.

The manager should resist the temptation to push the formal planning process to extremes. The deadly assumption of "if this works well, then more of this will work better" can easily lead to a paper mill and preoccupation with the plans themselves at the expense of the objectives. The reactions of the employees to the planning process can provide a fairly reliable indication of "how much is enough"—once they have become accustomed to the careful thinking and discipline which planning requires.

Monologues, Dialogues, and "Multilogues"

As the foregoing example shows, effective work planning within a group usually requires an ongoing process of communication between the manager and the group members and among the group members themselves. We can think of the kinds of communication processes as dictated largely by the kinds of objectives involved. In some cases, the manager may establish an objective—usually short-range, operational, and of self-evident value—and simply instruct an employee to do the work necessary to achieve it.

If the objective meets the five basic SPIRO criteria (Specific, Performance-oriented, Intrinsically rewarding, Realistic, and Observable), a direct order will probably suffice to get the employee on the proper track. We can consider this a "monologue" form of objective setting and planning. The manager should, of course, use effective communication techniques such as getting feedback and clarifying the instruction as necessary. But the sense of direction is fundamentally one way. This is an exercise of the manager's basic prerogative of command.

In many situations, however, the manager may have discovered a problem or an opportunity which invites attention but may not have clarified it sufficiently to direct action. In such a case, a "dialogue" form of objective setting and planning will usually lead to a more effective solution than the manager could achieve by struggling with the problem alone and finally giving a direct order. The manager can discuss the problem with the employee, trading perspectives, opinions, and factual information until they have jointly clarified the issue. This discussion can lead to a statement of objectives which both manager and employee feel will constitute a solution. The dialogue approach has the advantage of enriching the manager's point of view on the problem or opportunity. It also generally wins the enthusiastic support of the employee in achieving the objective, because of the automatic sense of "ownership" which the dialogue approach confers.

In other situations, the manager will need to draw upon the combined expertise and perspectives of several employees, or even all of them in certain situations. A group discussion of the problem of opportunity, chaired by the manager, can clarify the issue and surface possible objectives for consideration. With the manager's guidance, the group can settle on one or more objectives which the members feel constitute a reasonable solution. This "multilogue" process, if managed well, can lead to effective solutions which have the full support of group members and which they themselves own. Then the manager can assign one lead person to spearhead the project, with the understanding that each of the others will contribute as appropriate. A brief written plan for the project will state the agreed objectives, identify responsible people, spell out their various activities, and give deadlines for the various accomplishments.

To a very great extent, skill in managing by objectives means skill in communicating in a variety of directions, on a variety of topics. The manager's interpersonal style plays an important part in the success of the problem-solving, objective-setting, and planning process. To maintain a high level of employee involvement and commitment, the manager must achieve a comfortable balance among monologue, dialogue, and multilogue approaches. Ultimate responsibility rests with the manager, of course, but most of the operational knowledge, day-to-day perspective on work activities, and ideas for improvement usually reside with the employees themselves. Capitalizing on these resources requires a highly developed skill in communicating.

Defining Jobs in Performance Terms

By communicating in terms of objectives and by planning the work of the unit in cooperation with the employees, the manager can make a general policy of defining jobs in terms of performance. Although direct instruction is still appropriate for a certain proportion of managerial guidance, the manager can create greater freedom for all members of the group by focusing on *what* is to be done, not on *how* it is to be done. The unit's planning process should support this policy, and the day-to-day work activities should result from it. This combination of routinely assigned duties and specifically assigned projects will usually suffice to give each employee a sense of knowing what the manager expects and how to achieve it. This feeling alone can serve as a powerful source of employee involvement and commitment. Virtually every worker likes to know what constitutes a good job and to feel that he can do it.

Some jobs, however, do not lend themselves easily to an equilibrium definition of routine duties. In fact, some kinds of jobs require the employee to define the tasks for himself within very broad guidelines. An example of such a job is the position of marketer for grant projects. This person's task is to find sponsors for research activities. Other examples are the jobs of an affirmative-action officer in a large corporation and a research scientist in a high-technology department who is exploring a relatively unknown area. In these cases, the manager lacks the direct contact with the employee's situation to give specific instruction or to define the job as a matter of routine. He must rely on the employee to be self-motivating and self-directing by virtue of specific expertise and general maturity. The manager and the employee in this situation need a common form of communication which will enable them to settle on objectives and a general approach by which the employee will try to achieve them. Setting workable objectives in many such cases may offer an enormous challenge to the manager and the employee, but without at least a general statement of objectives, neither of them will have a clear idea whether the job is worth doing at all.

A useful technique for managing these kinds of jobs is the *individual job plan*. Instead of writing the conventional "job description," which specifies typical activities in a relatively static—and often vague—format, the employee and the manager confer to develop a plan for the employee's individual contribution to the unit's work. A job plan can spell out several key result areas which constitute the employee's overall job. Within each of these result areas, the employee can propose for managerial approval one or more specific objectives. This has the effect of focusing their attention on payoffs and creating a framework within which the employee can plan day-to-day activities.

A typical job plan is from one to three pages long. It is not especially formalized, but it does give clearly stated objectives and a timetable for their achievement. The plan might cover three months, six months, a year, or any other convenient planning period. The plan should use very simple, straightforward language. It should focus on what the employee expects to achieve and should not deal with specific activities unless they are critical to achieving the objectives.

Having considered the matter of plans and programs from the manager's point of view, let's see how the management-by-objectives approach works for the employee. The philosophy of defining as much of the employee's job as possible in performance terms leads to a hierarchy of managerial guidance tailored to the employee's individual needs. A typical employee would spend a certain fraction of the day carrying out routine work according to well-understood responsibilities and job standards. If the job is very complex and changeable, the employee will have an individual job plan which specifies objectives for some practical planning period. And finally, the employee will devote some time to the objectives of a specific project plan previously worked out in cooperation with the manager. The situation should also allow at least a small portion of time which the employee is free to allocate to unexpected problems, new ideas, and self-development within the job.

In the objectives-oriented environment, every worker becomes a kind of entrepreneur, working in a self-directed way toward worthwhile objectives. This approach of using objectives liberates the manager as well as the employees and enables both to use their energies effectively for the benefit of the organization.

Setting Achievable
Performance Goals

The notion of defining jobs in performance terms brings us to one of the most important questions of all: How high should the employee's objectives be? What constitutes the "realistic" portion of the SPIRO recipe for goal setting?

I disagree emphatically with most of the prominent management writers on this crucial point, so I take this opportunity to advance my own point of view. Paul Mali, George Odiorne, and a number of other writers contend that the objective should be "challenging" for the employee. That is, the manager should influence the employee during the objective-setting discussion to embrace an objective which will stretch the employee's capacities somewhat. I agree with the notion of challenging the employee, but I believe these distinguished gentlemen have overlooked a very fundamental point.

Mali's notion of a challenging objective, for example, calls for a measureable goal which offers considerably less than 100 percent probability of attainment.[2] He describes the range of possible values for the goal in question in terms of a normal probability distribution. He labels the lower end of the performance scale the "marginal" region. The middle sector becomes the "average" region, and the upper sector becomes the "challenge" region. Mali contends that a goal should lie within the challenge region; i.e., it should present some difficulty for the employee in achieving it. He acknowledges that this policy leads to a substantial number of "misses"—cases where the employee falls somewhat short of the planned goal.

Similarly, a U.S. Government publication states:

> If an organization is consistently accomplishing 100 percent of its objectives, there is probably reason for concern rather than celebration. Objectives are not really effective unless an organization must "stretch" to reach them. During the last fiscal year, for example, approximately one-fourth of HEW's objectives were only partially achieved and another one-eighth fell far short of expectation. This is probably not an unhealthy balance.[3]

[2]Paul Mali, *Managing by Objectives* (New York: John Wiley & Sons, 1972), p. 135.
[3]Mark L. McConkie, *Management by Objectives: a Corrections Perspective* (Washington, D.C.: U.S. Department of Justice), p. 31.

I believe these writers have missed a very serious point, and I have no doubt that the organizations involved suffer the consequences of the oversight. That point is that the morale, motivation, and commitment of the workers in an organization *depends upon a sense of achievement.* If the organization's managers rig the game in such a way that many people derive a sense of failure or shortfall, in order for a few of them to reward the managers with impressive results, then they have thrown away the one essential ingredient of organizational health—the commitment of the organization's general population.

People derive good feelings from succeeding, not from "almost succeeding." Two common expressions in the American lexicon tell the tale. They are "A miss is as good as a mile," and "Nothing succeeds like success." I believe that every manager has a golden opportunity to foster high morale and employee commitment by rigging the game in favor of success. While I don't advocate setting goals so low that their attainment becomes trivial and unrewarding, I believe that *achieving objectives should be the general norm, rather than the exception.* This notion of favoring success on the part of the employees flies directly in the face of our traditional Puritan ethic, which implies that people are fundamentally evil and must suffer if they are ever to improve themselves. Given the traditional pre-war view of work as something which is not supposed to be enjoyable, and the general preoccupation of American managers with performance at any cost, we can see why many employees in many organizations harbor suspicion and resentment toward "management by objectives" as they know it. There's very little in it *for them.*

But the notion of favoring successful employee performance bears directly on the issue of long-run organizational performance. Just as one can choose to go around a mountain rather over it, so the manager can choose to build organizational performance by building employee feelings of accomplishment, competence, pride in achievement, and commitment to the organization as a good place to live and work.

This issue of how high to set goals presents itself forcefully during the period when an organization's managers are first trying to bring management by objectives into the organization as an overall philosophy. If the first experiment with objectives-oriented working results in feelings of frustration, inadequacy, and failure to achieve the goals, then the entire process may be doomed. The inevitable confusion caused by a new approach to life will present enormous difficulties in and of itself. Adding a sense of "challenge" to this already threatening situation may very well sink the ship. And, indeed, this is what we see in many organizations which install so-called MBO programs.

Conversely, if the employees get the idea this new approach to working offers opportunities to succeed and to gain recognition for their efforts, how are they likely to respond to the change? The answer is obvious. If the organization's managers can set aside their own needs for a sense of impact and focus on the employees' needs for a sense of self-esteem through accomplishment, then they can design the entire program to foster involvement and commitment. So far as we know, this is the one essential ingredient for long-term success in managing by objectives.

Appraising Performance

The process of appraising performance should flow naturally from the problem-solving and goal-setting process, and from the day-to-day performance of the work. Yet, in many organizations the two are disconnected. Or even worse, some managers set up so-called "MBO systems" for the sole purpose of evaluating employees. Performance appraisal has created more consternation than perhaps any other single issue in American management. Organizational approaches to performance appraisal typically range from dismal to mediocre, with a very few verging on the excellent.

Simply stated, the problem is that most managers do not really appraise performance; they find themselves attempting to evaluate the individual as a person. This case of mistaken identity has caused a great deal of frustration, disappointment, hard feelings, and even formal grievances. Some organizations have no formal process for appraising performance. Others have formal processes which no one follows. Still others have formal processes administered by the managers themselves.

In a typical large organization, the manager receives a yearly form to fill out, asking for an "appraisal" of one or more of the employees. The form may give abstract qualities such as "initiative," "loyalty," "technical competence," or "cooperativeness." If the manager gets along well with the particular employee, he rates the individual as "outstanding" in most of the categories, reserving a few ratings of "high" to show that nobody is perfect. The employee reads it and signs it, and the annual ritual is complete. If the two do not get along very well together, this is the manager's opportunity to gently rap the employee's knuckles or even to seriously jeopardize his job tenure. If the employee chooses to do battle, he can add his own comments and ask for higher-level review. Unfortunately, both parties usually see the appraisal process as irrelevant to their effectiveness in getting their jobs done. At best, the appraisal form offers a weapon in case they choose to engage in a power struggle. For many managers, the annual appraisal is the only time when they sit down privately with an individual employee and discuss performance on a person-to-person basis. Many managers find this personal aspect of their jobs frightening and anxiety-producing. Employees working for these managers seldom solicit a performance interview, for fear of getting bad news. The typical manager-employee compromise calls for continuing to drift along unless problems arise.

Another aspect of the appraisal process, which management theorists seldom recognize, is the ritual affirmation of the unit manager's authority. This has little to do with employee performance or individual motivation, but many managers find it a comfortable reminder of their status. However, it offers very little help to the manager or the employee in communicating about goals, accomplishment, and rewards.

Organizations have traditionally tied the performance-appraisal process to the annual salary review, making it a time for anxiety and guarded behavior rather than an opportunity for relaxed and open discussion. This puts the manager in the position of doling out "jelly beans" in exchange for a very generalized form of employee behavior over the previous review period. If the manager has a generally cool and distant interpersonal style, with little inclination to offer psychological rewards on a day-to-day basis, the employee may come to see the annual salary review as the only opportunity to get a reward for past work. With the conventional normative limits on salary increases within most organizations, this is not likely to be a momentous point in the employee's life. Traditionally, the psychological effect of a salary increase wears off within about two pay periods.

With a management-by-objectives approach, the manager and the employee jointly *appraise the performance, not the person.* As part of their ongoing interaction, they focus their attention on the objectives, and on progress toward them. By a continual process of re-evaluation and replanning, they keep their expectations reasonable with respect to the problems and opportunities facing them. And at certain specified times, they can choose to discuss the employee's job, career, past accomplishments, interests, ideas, preferences, and needs for development, within the context of the job situation. In this case, they focus on behavior instead of personality traits, and they deal with the future.

It may help to clarify the appraisal issue by thinking in terms of *potential* rather than past performance. By the time the manager and the employee meet to formally review progress, they are discussing "history." Whatever the employee has or has not accomplished is now in the past. Rather than focus on the past, the manager can focus on future possibilities. Indeed, the manager must decide in any case what kinds of assignments the employee will be able to handle, what kinds of challenges to offer, and how much autonomy to grant. The manager must consider past performance in deciding these questions, but there is little value in agonizing over past mistakes and shortcomings.

Except in those relatively few cases when the employee's behavior presents serious problems, the manager and the employee should jointly look ahead to their next planning period and discuss objectives and means for achieving them. This gives a sense of a continuous process rather than a periodic event. During the review process, both manager and employee can deal frankly with any needs for personal development the employee may have. The review thus becomes a time for constructive planning and goal setting, rather than holding trial.

The performance review also provides an often overlooked opportunity for building morale and motivation on the part of the employee. If the manager and the employee have previously worked out achievable objectives, then most probably the employee can come to the review meeting with a feeling of confidence and pride in having accomplished worthwhile results. This will automatically give the discussion a positive orientation. The manager can sincerely acknowledge a job well done. With this kind of affirmation, the employee will come away from the meeting with a feeling of being appreciated and a new sense of enthusiasm.

This is a far cry from the traditional review situation, which places the manager in a wager with the employee—betting that the employee will not have met the objectives and prepared to mete out punishment (or withhold rewards) for this. The employee, meanwhile, has bet that his performance will fall within the acceptable range and that he will come out of the review meeting unscathed. While the punitive manager uses the review for a display of authority and an opportunity to sit in judgement of the employee, the enlightened objectives-oriented manager uses it as an opportunity for giving encouragement and building employee commitment to the unit's effectiveness. These concepts of performance appraisal apply just as well to the appraisal of a manager by his boss as they apply to his appraisal of his own employees. A manager has the same needs as any other employee for job satisfaction, a sense of accomplishment, a feeling of support and encouragement from the boss, and the security of knowing what a good job really is and how to do it. When an executive meets with a subordinate manager to appraise performance, the two of them need the same basis for discussion as the subordinate manager needs in meeting with his employees. They need agreed-upon objectives, a clear idea of achieved results, and a clear idea of future possibilities.

All of the foregoing factors point clearly to a new concept of the performance appraisal. Appraising performance should not be an isolated "extra duty" for the manager, characterized by filling out a form and rushing through an uncomfortable and embarrassing five-minute meeting with the employee. *It should be an integrated element of the entire process of managing.* Just as the manager and the employee confer frequently to analyze problems, review opportunities, arrive at solutions, and set objectives, so also must they confer about results, analyze their progress, revise expectations as necessary, and renew their thinking. Within this continual process, the manager must pay attention to the matter of employee involvement, motivation, and commitment, as a fundamental part of managing. When they meet to appraise performance, they are really appraising themselves as a team, not merely the employee as an independent agent. If the manager-employee relationship has been a rewarding one, then appraisal can be a positive, uplifting experience for both of them.

9

Systems and Methods

The "system sciences" have many useful tools to offer the objectives-oriented manager. These tools can help to organize information, facilitate problem solving, help in communicating objectives, and help in making objectives come together in a practical, realistic plan for managing. This chapter highlights a few of the more interesting tools and techniques and discusses their application in managing by objectives.[1]

Keeping It Simple

A continual theme throughout this book has been *"keep it simple."* For reasons which must now be clear, the objectives-oriented manager uses formal plans, systems, and methods only to the extent that they help to get the organization's work done. The effective manager never allows the tools and techniques of managing to become more important than freedom of choice, flexibility, and professional judgement. If we keep our attention focused on management by objectives as a well-defined behavior pattern, rather than any one method or paper system, then we will avoid most of the pitfalls which have lured managers toward disaster as they have tried to build so-called MBO systems.

[1]For a thorough treatment of management tools, see Richard Levin and Charles Kirkpatrick, *Quantitative Approaches to Management* (New York: McGraw-Hill Book Company, 1965).

Any systematic management tool, if it is to be helpful, should meet a few very important criteria:

1. It should be simple; the employees should find it easy to understand and work with; the manager should find it easy to apply to the job of managing.
2. It should require very little time in and of itself; it must provide a useful advantage without requiring an unreasonable amount of time from either the manager or the employees.
3. It should be effective; that is, it should contribute something significant to the unit's business rather than just the appearance of order and method.
4. It should be "natural"—i.e., it should fit in with the business of managing and with working in such a way that seems to be an integral part of the process to which it applies.

With these criteria in mind, let's review some useful systems tools.

The Key-Result-Area Model

The Key-Result-Area model helps the manager and the employees deal with all major aspects of the unit's business when they think about about their objectives. In order to concentrate their resources within a few areas of relatively high payoff, they must identify the major dimensions of their endeavor and decide what they want to achieve in each of these dimensions. The diagram in Figure 9-1 shows how to model the selected "KRA's" as a unified whole. The dimensions of this particular example represent some of the key interests of an industrial company. Another kind of an organization might have various other KRA's unique to its operation. Just having such a simple diagram can help the manager immensely in assessing the organization's performance and in selecting areas for concentration in goal setting. This model makes a useful wall chart which will remind the manager and the employees of the major dimensions of the unit's operation.

The Key-Result-Area model can also provide you as a manager with a tool for your own self-development. You may choose to work out a personal system of goals, considering areas such as Professional, Financial, Social, Family, Creative, Cultural, Recreational, and Health. By looking at these Key Result Areas as a system, you are dealing with your life as a unified process. You can establish goals and priorities for your life and your career just as you do for the operation of your organization.

Another useful application of the KRA model involves sketching out the radial diagram as shown in the figure and marking a big dot on each

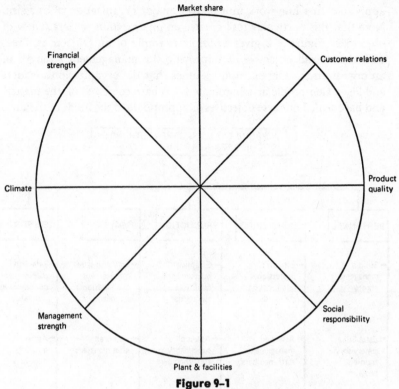

Figure 9–1
Key-Result-Area Model

axis at a distance from the center which represents the relative priority you choose to give to each area in the coming period. A dot placed near the circumference of the wheel can indicate a high priority for that area relative to the others. A dot placed close to the center indicates a relative degree of satisfaction with that particular area compared to others which need more attention and emphasis in goal setting.

The Objectives Tree

When a major organizational effort requires integration of the contributions of a variety of its subunits, the Objectives Tree provides a useful way to interrelate the various subobjectives. This process of subdividing an overall objective into specific contributing objectives can apply to a first-line work unit or to a major organization of any size. Note that this particular tool creates an *organization-centered* view of objectives. Figure 9-2 gives a simple example of an Objectives Tree, with the overall objective of improving the management strength of an organization. The example assumes that the organization's leaders and key action-people at subordinate levels have conferred on the matter, and have settled on these objectives as appropriate to the needs of the unit.

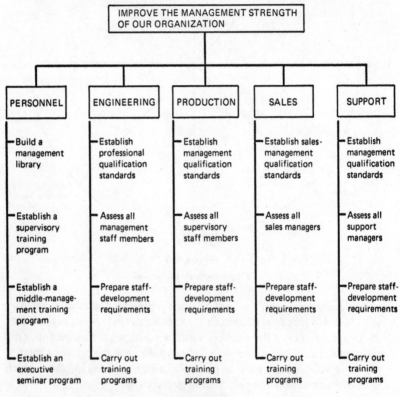

Figure 9-2
The Objective Tree

The heads of each of the responsible departments would prepare formal plans for achieving their objectives. They would coordinate their efforts to the extent necessary to ensure that all the activities blend together into a unified program for achieving the top-level objective. Note that, in this example, the top-level objective is stated in fuzzy form. Note further that we could call the subunit statements "activities," if we chose, rather than objectives. But for the purposes of the managers in this example, these may just as legitimately serve as objectives, because they represent a combined approach to managing the organization which the managers believe will bring desired payoffs. We need not demand that this particular model specify each objective down to the last detail, provided we are satisfied that the various departmental action plans do specify them adequately. The Objectives Tree usually serves best as a general overview of the breakdown of a major organizational objective. The degree of detail it provides will usually depend on the nature of the overall objective and on the number of subdivisions of the effort required to achieve it. The Objectives Tree can portray an indefinite number of subdivisions and subsequent levels. But two or three levels usually suffice to give a clear overview of the project and to show how the various departments or key people will carry it out.

The Work-Breakdown Structure

The Work-Breakdown Structure model gives a complete picture of the specific activities required to meet a top-level objective. This arrangement focuses on the natural subdivisions of the work itself, rather than on the organizational units which all accomplish it. The model is useful when so many of the activities involve more than one unit such that a simple Objectives Tree would not give the necessary emphasis on integration.

Figure 9–3 shows the basic form of the Work-Breakdown Structure model for the example of activating a new department within an organization. The model might serve as a useful adjunct to the top manager's project plan for the activation. It would help the manager and the staff to account for all of the many activities, large and small, involved in the activation, and to ensure that they complete them all. Note that this particular tool creates a *task-centered* picture of the objectives.

The work breakdown can extend to any desired level of detail. The appropriate level usually depends on the magnitude of the project and the relative number and complexity of the activities involved. The number of people and organizations involved can also affect the choice of levels. As a general policy, the project manager should subdivide the work down to that level which clearly shows specific individuals or individual units as responsible for their completion. Then the Work-

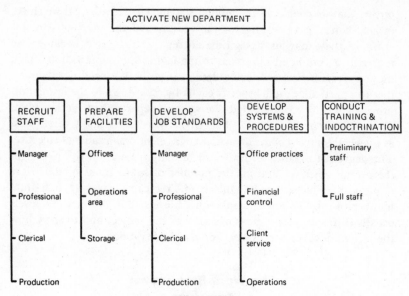

Figure 9–3
The Work-Breakdown Structure Model

Breakdown Structure becomes an accountability model, which enables the manager to follow up on each task without confusion about who has the responsibility.

The Activity Network

The Activity-Network model shows the various key activities required to achieve an overall objective, emphasizing the time dependence of certain activities upon others. If the various project activities require a great degree of coordination, and if certain activities cannot proceed until others have been completed, then the Activity Network can provide a clear picture of the overall effort and a general understanding of the timing of the final objective.

Figure 9-4 shows a simple Activity Network for the example of opening up a small field office in a foreign city. Note that some activities simply cannot proceed without the successful completion of others. This aspect of the diagram focuses our attention strongly on several key activities as high-priority items for attention. If they proceed smoothly, then we

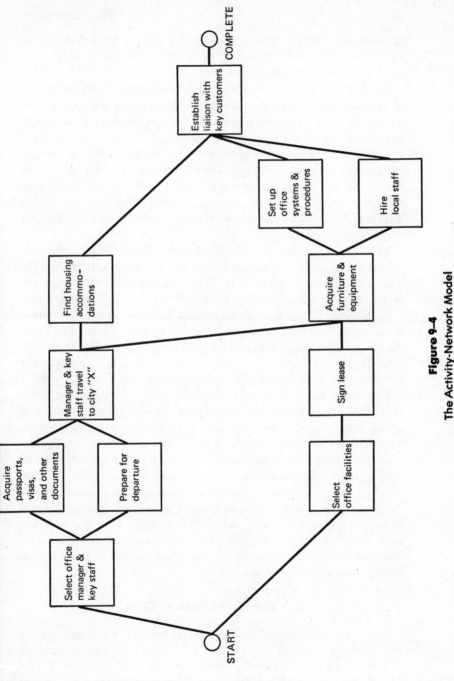

Figure 9-4
The Activity-Network Model

can meet the overall objective. But if they become bogged down, we must act quickly and energetically to get them completed, so they will not impose unacceptable delays on other activities.

The Activity Network provides a tool for studying the interrelationships of key activities up to a thousand or more elements. Very large-scale projects usually require extensive analysis and diagramming of the various activities, as well as a great deal of monitoring and evaluation of ongoing status. The larger the project, of course, the more effort it will require in monitoring and controlling it. The manager of a multimillion-dollar project will typically have at least a few assistants who provide continuous support in trouble shooting, status monitoring, and reporting on key activities. The Activity Network serves as the starting point for this kind of project management.

The *"critical path"* concept associated with the Activity Network provides a convenient yardstick for project monitoring. It enables the manager to focus attention on those few activities which dominate the success of the project, in terms of completion time and the associated costs. The critical path through the network is that sequence of activities— of the many possible paths from beginning to end—which adds up to the longest time period for completion. This defines the fastest possible schedule for achieving the objective, since all of the activities along the path contribute sequentially to the elapsed time.

You can draw an Activity Network for accomplishing an objective very simply. Just list all of the known activities which must proceed and group them roughly into convenient categories or parallel sequences. Then sketch them out along a time scale, arranging them in sequence. Draw connecting lines when necessary to show that one activity "enables" another—i.e., that the second cannot proceed before the first finishes. You may need to redraw the network more neatly after you have worked out the various dependencies, in order to avoid intersecting lines and to convey a general sense of timing. Then simply write the expected time requirement for each activity in its own box on the diagram. You can then find the critical path and call attention to it with heavy lines or some distinctive color if you choose.

The Master-Milestone Chart

The Master-Milestone Chart gives a simple and convenient picture of the time phasing of a major objective. It shows a series of intermediate objectives called "milestones" and diagrams their relationships. Figure 9-5 shows a typical Master-Milestone Chart for the example of a new

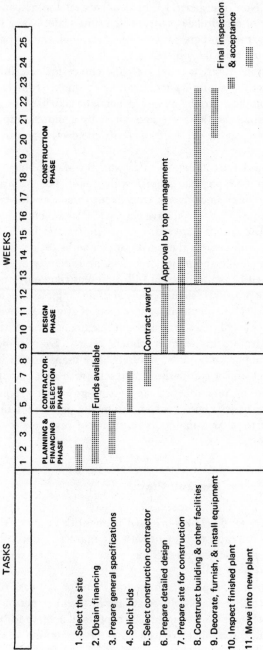

Figure 9–5
Master-Milestone Chart

plant construction. Note the general time sequence of the activities, and the prominence of certain key points on the time scale. These key points, or milestones, mark progress toward the overall objective. Each represents a distinct intermediate objective.

The Master-Milestone Chart is usually a good choice for describing a project when the activities form a generally linear sequence from start to finish, without complex parallel or interdependent activities. It can also serve to summarize the flow of events given by a more complex activity network. Both models can help to clarify the overall approach to achieving the objective.

By adhering to a few basic conventions in drawing the Master-Milestone Chart, you can keep it simple and operationally useful. For example, spread the various activities out over a convenient time scale for easy reading. Label the time intervals you have chosen and show actual dates whenever possible. Use straightforward, easy-to-understand labels for the various activities and express them with action verbs. Select a few key points along the way to the major objective, and identify these as key milestones. A well-chosen milestone will represent the completion of a major step in the project. It should result in some tangible evidence of accomplishment, such as a physical event or state of affairs, the availability of a written report of other management document, or a written statement resulting from a major management review. Every project milestone offers an opportunity for a comprehensive management appraisal of the project and a comparison of results with expectations. One important kind of milestone is the "go/no-go" review point, where the project manager reviews accomplishments up to that time and decides whether to make a major commitment of resources to the next phase of the effort.

The Job Plan

The Job Plan offers an objectives-oriented framework for specifying an employee's needs to reach agreement with the manager concerning key results expected and the general method for achieving these results. The Job Plan serves this need.

Exhibit 9-1 gives an example of a brief Job Plan for the case of a market analyst. Note that the employee speaks in the first person in this example and spells out the objectives she expects to achieve for the year. This plan would probably serve as a basis for a planning session between the manager and the market analyst. If the manager deems the goals reasonable and the plan worthwhile, the employee can then begin working toward the goals. After this go-ahead, the manager can expect the employee to accomplish the goals unless she encounters unusual problems, and the employee has a right to expect the manager's support and acknowledgment of the goals as the basis for her day-to-day work.

The Job Plan provides an excellent means for gaining employee commitment to worthwhile goals. The employee who proposes the goals for his own job can generally be expected to work toward them with a high level of commitment. The manager will usually not need to do any more than keep in regular contact with the employee, discussing progress and offering assistance as needed. Other routine aspects of day-to-day business will fall into line according to a reasonable system of priorities, ensuring that they do not interfere too much with the allocation of energies toward the desired goals.

Exhibit 9-1
The Job Plan

January 1, 19   to December 31, 19

NAME: Mary Doe

JOB: Market Analyst, Packaging-Materials Division

KEY RESULT AREAS FOR THIS YEAR:

1. *Price Analysis*—During this year, I will conduct an intensive analysis of our competitors' pricing structures and will publish written reports to serve the needs of our market-planning staff. By March 31, I will have completed and published reports on Companies A and B. By June 30, I will have added reports on the six remaining competitors of direct interest to our marketing efforts. By the end of the year, I will have updated all reports and will have them fully available to all key individuals throughout the division, in addition to the market-planning staff.

2. *Materials Availability*—By the end of each quarter of this year, I will publish a comprehensive report on availability and pricing of our major raw materials for the just-finished quarter.

3. *Long-Term Trends Study*—By the end of June, I will have completed a comparative study of long-term trends in the packaging of snack-food items, with emphasis on management planning and market strategy. I will have prepared the results of the study in draft form by July 31, and if management review and acceptance of the report follows within two weeks, I will publish the report for general use by August 31.

ROUTINE DUTIES:

1. Consult with members of the market-planning staff on technical questions—
   estimated two hours per week.
2. Continue to develop and maintain market-research library—estimated
   four hours per week.
3. Attend training seminars and professional conferences within my field
   of specialization—estimated two hours per week.
4. Prepare market briefs and technical memoranda as requested—estimated
   ten hours per week.

PERSONAL OBJECTIVES:

1. I expect to complete the requirements for my Master's degree in operations research and to receive the degree before the end of the year.
2. I expect to become eligible for promotion to Senior Market Analyst by
   the end of this year.

The Daily Time-Management Worksheet

The Time-Management Worksheet is an invaluable tool for helping
any manager, in any situation, to maintain a habit of objectives-oriented
working. It is merely a list of things to do, with every item of significance
included, and with every item earmarked to indicate its relative priority.

Figure 9-6 shows a typical Time-Management Worksheet, arranged
for weekly planning as well as for long-term "visibility" of up-coming
actions. This is, of course, merely one arrangement of the list of things
to do. Try this and other possible arrangements to find one which fits
your needs best. You can make the Time-Management Worksheet a
daily basis for allocating your time, for deciding what to do and when.
Have a number of blank worksheets reproduced and begin using them.
At a convenient time, say each Monday morning, you can review the
upcoming demands of the week and add items to the list which you
plan to do. Cross off any completed items and use a fresh sheet if the
current one has become cluttered with crossed-off entries. For each
item you plan to do this week, assign it a priority level by checking the
appropriate rating—i.e., "Low," "Medium," or "High."

At various times during your day, you can then refer to the worksheet
to help you decide how to allocate your time. And, especially, the work-

TIME-MANAGEMENT WORKSHEET

THINGS TO DO THIS WEEK	PRIORITY (Circle one)			NOTES:
	HIGH	MEDIUM	LOW	
1.	H	M	L	
2.	H	M	L	
3.	H	M	L	
4.	H	M	L	
5.	H	M	L	
6.	H	M	L	
7.	H	M	L	
8.	H	M	L	
9.	H	M	L	
10.	H	M	L	
11.	H	M	L	
12.	H	M	L	
13.	H	M	L	
14.	H	M	L	
15.	H	M	L	
16.	H	M	L	
17.	H	M	L	
18.	H	M	L	
19.	H	M	L	
20.	H	M	L	
21.	H	M	L	
22.	H	M	L	
23.	H	M	L	
24.	H	M	L	
25.	H	M	L	

Figure 9–6
Daily Time-Management Worksheet

sheet will help you keep your attention focused on those high-payoff items you want to achieve, and to defend your time against the encroachments of lower-priority items as well as outright time-wasters.

The Decision Tree

The Decision Tree, a commonly used model within the systems sciences, enables the objectives-oriented manager to analyze problems and arrive at decisions which offer the greatest potential for accomplishing recognized objectives. The Decision Tree classifies the known options for the decision in question and displays them in a pictorial form which clarifies the overall issue. Figure 9-7 shows a Decision Tree for the example of a scheduling decision. In this hypothetical case, the manager must decide how to proceed after discovering that a major project within the unit has fallen behind schedule. Note that the Decision Tree presents all of the plausible options at a glance. The manager can evaluate each of them thoroughly and methodically by first specifying *the objectives of the decision*. That is, the manager must deal with the problem of project slippage in terms of realistic "wants," i.e., "What do I want from this particular situation?" The answer to this question will take the form of a goal or a set of goals which the "best" decision must enable the manager to achieve. Typical goals might be "continued good will of the client agency" (specified in reasonably observable terms), "completion of the project by X date," "project personnel costs not exceeding Y dollars," or "guaranteed achievement of all project objectives." The decision objectives must not be confused with the objectives of the project discussed in this particular example. One decision objective might be to accomplish all of the project objectives. An alternative decision objective, such as cost control, might require the abandonment of one or more project objectives.

After settling on the decision objectives, the manager then evaluates each of the options shown by the Decision Tree in terms of the extent to which they promise to meet the decision objectives. If the objectives reflect all relevant decision factors, then the "best" option will be the one that meets them most effectively.

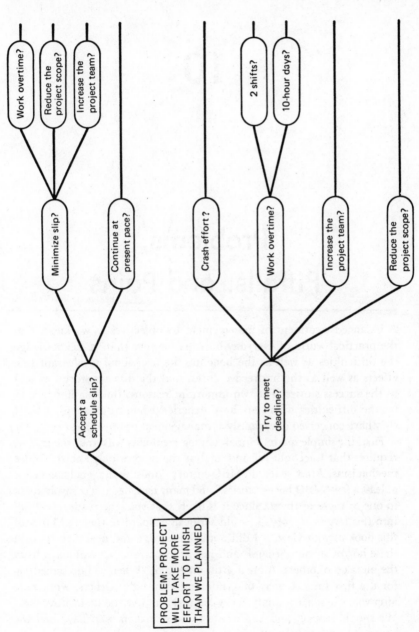

Figure 9-7
The Decision Tree

171

10

Problems,
Pitfalls, and Pains

A balanced treatment of management by objectives as we know it in the practical world of everyday business requires that we acknowledge the difficulties as well as the benefits, the occasional unpleasant side effects as well as the impressive cures, and the disaster stories as well as the success stories. For two important reasons, this chapter focuses on the difficulties managers have experienced in implementing what they have conceived of variously as management by objectives.

First, the simple matter of maintaining credibility with you, the reader, requires that I account for and analyze the more widely known failure mechanisms. After years of "MBO history," most managers have heard at least a few "MBO horror stories," and many have had direct involvement in one or more of them. Since it is likely that you, the reader, will fall into this large category, I would seriously jeopardize the credibility of this book in your view, if I did not acknowledge and deal directly with these horror stories. Second, and just as important, we can learn from the mistakes of others. A great artist once said, "When you do something for the first time, it may be crude and even ugly. Others, who come after you, can make it pretty. They can make it nicer and more attractive." We should respect and appreciate those managers who have had the courage to experiment, to try new ways of managing, to risk disaster while striving for managerial excellence. And for our own part we can balance the previous quoted message with another well-known maxim: "Those who will not learn from history are obliged to repeat it." One of the basic purposes of this book is to help as many managers as possible to avoid repeating history.[1]

The One Key Success Factor

As we have seen, many factors contribute to organizational performance. And managerial excellence, the principal topic of this book, forms the foundation for that performance. By creating and maintaining a reward-centered environment, by adopting objectives-oriented patterns of behavior, by teaching the employees to work in an objectives-oriented way, and by stepping up to the demanding roles of Strategist, Problem Solver, Leader, and Teacher, the manager helps ordinary people to achieve extraordinary things.

But of all the "success factors"; of all the wise decisions, lucky breaks, well-timed maneuvers, organizational advantages, special strong points, strong product lines, and the rest, one key factor seems to stand out as fundamental to the success of management by objectives as an organizational methodology. Those who have tried to make management by objectives a broad-scale approach to the organization's operation have repeatedly found that *employee commitment* has been the principal axis upon which all other success factors have turned. Commitment— the attitude of the organization's general population toward the organization as an abstract entity, toward their top managers, toward the work itself, and toward the physical and social environments in which they work every day—seems to exert an overwhelmingly important influence on achievement. Without it, the most creative and sophisticated plans and programs of its top managers don't seem to get far. With it, the most modest plan and the most straightforward programs seem to come out well.

Of course, it has been customary for chief executives to say, as if they really meant it, things like: "Our organization is people; without them, we could never accomplish anything; people are our most important resource, etc. etc." Especially since the coming of age of our high-speed public relations media, this has become the *sine qua non* of top-manage-

---

[1]Dale D. McConkey, "Twenty Ways to Kill Management by Objectives," *Management Review* (October, 1972), pp. 4–13. Karl Albrecht, "Managing by Objectives; or, How Not to Create a Monster," *Manage* (November–December, 1975).

ment pronouncements. Some chief executives manage their organizations as if they truly believe these principles. But it appears that most do not. That is, most organizations do not show the kinds of ecological "quality" of working life within their structures which are implied by the chief executives' remarks.

It appears that the majority of "MBO" failures—as defined by the eventual abandonment of the program by top management, or its eventual subversion and sabotage by the employees—have resulted fairly directly and fairly predictably from the members of the top-management team assuming that employee commitment would automatically come for free, instead of creating a foundation of employee commitment before initiating the project. In some cases, executives and middle managers have shown surprising naivete in overlooking the matter of employee commitment entirely.

All of the pitfalls discussed in this chapter relate more or less directly to the matter of commitment on the part of the organization's general population. They also connect fairly directly to the "management myths" described in Chapter 2. For example, the manager who holds a general view of employees as an undifferentiated rabble—the "Jackass Myth"— will probably resort to the stick and carrot treatment automatically, with little thought about how they might react as individuals to a new, unfamiliar, and confusing program imposed by management.

Similarly, the manager who falls prey to the "Machinery Myth" will probably assume that various "incidental" issues such as employee morale and acceptance of the changes imposed by management will get taken care of automatically somehow, by the magical workings of the well-oiled organizational machinery. This kind of manager's inability to perceive the organization as a human system stands in the way of important actions and compromises needed to make management by objectives work.

In the complex environment of American management, employee commitment may not be a sufficient condition for successful management by objectives, but it certainly is a necessary condition.

The *Rigor-Mortis* Trap

The *Rigor-Mortis* Trap results when a manager or a group of managers decide to "tighten up" the organization by "installing an MBO system." This is the consequence of the pendulum effect described in Chapter 2. When we find an organization at this end of the pendulum's swing, we see an overcontrolled Activity Trap. This is organizational *Rigor Mortis*.

Such an organization still has little sense of direction, but its managers enjoy strong feelings of "being in control." They have wall charts, status boards, "tickler" files or other follow-up schemes, and special assistants who keep the "MBO program" going. They have quarterly meetings to review progress toward objectives, they have annual objective-setting "seasons" which take a month or more to complete, and, above all, they have paper.

The managers preoccupy themselves with the form and function of the program as a matter of first importance and only secondarily with the actual achievements of the organization. Written objectives become a medium of exchange, moving about like so many pieces of private currency printed by the organization itself. The employees find it harder and harder to get the day's work done, due to the interfering requirements of writing objectives for tasks which previously were matters of routine and dialoguing objectives of many kinds with their supervisors.

In the *Rigor-Mortis* Trap, procedure replaces judgement. Legislation replaces creativity. Overcontrol and overdirection replace initiative. The previous state of disorganized confusion gives way to organized confusion. For a time, at least, the *Rigor-Mortis* situation reinforces itself. This happens for two reasons. First, the feelings of being in control and of having an impact on organizational processes keep the managers interested in the new "system" for some time, especially since its effects often do not become apparent for some time. During the "installation" phase the managers and employees of the organization expect, and are willing to tolerate, a certain amount of confusion and extra work. They will probably accept this without much complaint—unless the confusion period extends past the point at which they could reasonably expect the new system to reach equilibrium and function effectively.

Second, by reinforcing activity-trap behavior, the managers themselves generally shape the behavior of their employees according to their own needs for assurance. When the manager scolds an employee for failing to complete the "Weekly MBO Achievement Report," and fails to offer praise for a significant accomplishment which does not show up in the sheaf of "MBO Plans," the employee very quickly gets the message. The message, of course, says: "Help keep the MBO system going. This is Manager X's baby, and you had better support it. Get the other work done as best you can." When the manager praises the employees who always have their paper work in on time, the others quickly take the hint. The *Rigor-Mortis* Trap frequently cures itself, however, by eventually bringing about its own demise. When it becomes apparent that the new "MBO system" has failed to bring about the magical improvements which the organization's managers hoped for, and that it has actually caused more work and more confusion in the process, the managers begin to look around for ways to gracefully abandon it. If they cannot simplify the system, and convert its procedures into a more tolerable framework, they may simply jettison the entire mess. This process may involve a great deal of argument and unrest in the management circles, or it may simply lead to an unceremonious declaration from the chief executive. In any case, the decision to kill the program usually triggers a profound sense of relief among those who have been victimized in the performance of their everyday jobs. Statements like "Now we can get back to work!" and "I hope we never go through *that* again!" testify to the punishing effects of the *Rigor-Mortis* Trap on the organization's people and on their combined effectiveness.

The Paper Jungle

The Paper Jungle stems from a naive view of visibility and control on the part of the organization's managers. If they believe they must have detailed information on all organizational processes from the top to the bottom in order to manage by objectives, they will be tempted to demand quantities of data and varieties of reports which impose an unreasonable work load on the employees of the organization.

You can easily recognize the Paper Jungle. If you ask various managers within the organization to explain the "MBO system" to you, they will immediately reach for stacks of plans, reports, and analyses. They describe the system to you in terms of particular items of paper, because *they think of the system as a paper system.* Instead of focusing on the problems and opportunities facing the organization, they focus on their procedures for going about daily life. A typical well-developed Paper Jungle will have an "MBO Manual," which gives a detailed explanation of the "system," defines all the paper tools, and prescribes detailed procedures for manipulating them. There may also be supervisor's manuals, to make sure that all units comply with the new way of life. A large organization may have a special manual, published every year, giving corporate goals.

Branching out from the "MBO Manual," we may find a family of "MBO Plans," each addressing a separate area which someone in management considers important. These plans may then fan out to various subplans, which become the responsibility of specific individuals or work groups. And, of course, to support the plans we must have periodic "MBO Reports," which tell how well the employees have progressed on their individual plans. All of these will find their way into a composite "Annual MBO Report," prepared by a corporate officer who has the extra duty of keeping the paper system operating.

What's wrong with this situation? Simply that the maintenance of the paper system drains off too much of the time and energy which the employees need to get the work itself done. A frequent gripe heard from the underbrush of the Paper Jungle is, "If I didn't have to waste so much time writing up all of this stuff about how I'm going to get my work done, I could get my work done." Although many managers tend to dismiss this complaint as the "normal" grumbling of employees who "don't see the big picture," more often than not this comment provides a very accurate measure of the effectiveness—or lack of it—of the paper system.

Many Paper-Jungle managers have missed the basic principle of management by objectives, namely that people work well when they can aim their efforts toward worthwhile goals and when they know very clearly what their managers expect them to accomplish. These managers have tried to substitute a paper system for a thinking process. The result of trying to manage paper instead of people is uniformly disastrous.

The way out of the Paper Jungle is simply a return to basics. The managers must focus on those few key result areas which hold the greatest promise for organizational performance and build a set of simple objectives. Then they must communicate this sense of direction throughout the organization, allowing other action people to set implementing objectives and make plans as they see fit. They must call for *strategic visibility*—i.e., only that information necessary for top managers to do their jobs. Then they must grant the people of the organization enough autonomy to do the work.

Objectives for the Sake of Objectives

Occasionally, a manager will try to "wake up" an organization by handing out a batch of objectives, with the expectation that people will begin to work more effectively. Many times they do, but just as many times they become confused and disoriented by what they may perceive as a redirection of their efforts. Such a manager may have read one of the contemporary mechanistic books on MBO, or may have merely heard the term and postulated a reasonable-sounding theory based on skimpy information.

This approach seems to derive from the point of view that having objectives is fundamentally a good thing and that setting objectives requires only that the manager sit down one afternoon with a pad and pencil and make a list of good things which the people of the organization should accomplish. More often than not, these "objectives" come out as specific directions for action rather than as goals. Typical examples would include "Write ten grant proposals this year," or "Give two sales presentations per month to major clients," or "Issue one news release per month describing the Agency's activities in the area of Equal Employment Opportunity." These may very well be worthwhile things to do, but the manager should recognize that they constitute directives rather than objectives. The "want" originated with the manager, the thinking process stayed there, and the prescription of how to satisfy the want originated there. It remains only for the employees to carry out the instruction.

This indeed constitutes a redirection of the employees' efforts. In the absence of this kind of managerial specification, they would do their regular work. Given this new work requirement, most employees would willingly try to do what they believed the manager wanted them to do. In such a case, unfortunately, the employees do not "own" the objectives. They had little or no part to play in setting them, and they see them as merely extra items of work.

Without the benefit of a continuing dialogue between managers and employees about the organization's progress and about the things they want to accomplish, the managers cannot set very effective objectives. Managers who see their jobs as involving one-way interactions with their employees will usually fall into the trap of Objectives for the Sake of Objectives.

This particular pitfall may not cause as much harm as some of the other MBO pitfalls. In fact, it may even become the first phase of a gradually maturing managerial pattern of focusing on objectives. If the managers involved have a relatively long attention span, and if they appraise the results of their managing realistically, they will probably look more deeply into the organizational dynamics they are dealing with. They can learn to assess organizational performance, to establish a sense of direction and communicate it to the employees, and to guide their efforts toward realistic and worthwhile goals. Both employees and managers can use objectives as a way to communicate as well as a way to work.

The Self-Made Prison

The Self-Made Prison Trap stems from a rigid managerial attitude toward plans and planning. In this case, the manager makes a plan based on a current estimate of the future and of possible accomplishments and becomes enslaved to the plan. Sometimes this attitude spreads across an entire organization, making its members generally anxious about the process of planning and about accountability. The organization's managers may lay down broad objectives and direct that their subordinates define subobjectives and make plans for achieving them. This in itself may be a very effective step, especially if the objectives reflect a realistic view of the organization's needs and capabilities. So far, so good.

But occasionally, the managers forget that people are human, that everyone can make mistakes, that no one can foretell the exact future, that problems and unexpected events do arise, and that results do not always meet expectations. If they fasten on the original plans with a compulsive intensity and are unwilling to revise their expectations, then they will be tempted to try to "force" the employees to meet the objectives by threat of punishment and daily pressure. They may act as if the cause of failure to meet the objectives lies with the employees. Perhaps the employees don't work hard enough. Perhaps they don't really support the success of the organization. Perhaps they just don't work very well without having pressure applied to them by the managers.

An alternative—and equally plausible—point of view holds that the plan serves only as a communication device. The managers and the employees plan as well as they know how, and they write down the more important conclusions of their planning process, so they can keep their attention focused on accomplishment. But they must consider the planning process a continuing one, even though they might only republish the plan at specified intervals. If they ever let the plan become a graven image, or a sacred commandment, then they have fallen into their own Self-Made Prison.

Escape from the Self-Made Prison requires a revision of managerial attitudes about planning. A manager who refuses to plan realistically will inevitably be victimized by the plan. The more enlightened manager plans carefully and realistically—even ambitiously—and then refuses to take the plan too seriously. Such a manager expects changes, and expects to replan the effort to adapt to the changed circumstances. A realistic definition of a plan is *a sequence of intended actions in connection with a specific anticipated future.* The manager who can tell the difference between adequate employee performance and adequate planning seldom falls into the Self-Made Prison of enslavement to the plans themselves.

The Rat Race

The Rat-Race Trap, one of the most damaging and toxic situations possible in an organization, arises from managerial attempts to install an "MBO system" in the context of a punitive, Theory-X environment. For these people, "MBO" becomes a framework for handing out jelly beans on rare occasions and for meting out punishment on frequent occasions.

When managers conceive of employees as a generalized herd of cattle whom they must frighten, prod, and coerce into working, they tend to adopt the items of conventional management machinery which serve those purposes. Rat-Race managers give more attention to failure, shortcomings, and missed objectives than they give to success and achievement. They focus on punishment more than on reward.

The manager-employee relationship in the Rat-Race environment seems to take on an adversary orientation. They seem to be engaged in a wager wherein the employee bets on achieving a pre-established level of performance and the manager bets against it. From the employee's point of view such a game is rigged from the beginning. If the employee achieves the objective, he will receive a symbolic "check mark," or a "gold star." Come salary review time, a good score of these points—sometimes called "attaboys" by cynical employees—will mean that the manager will "look favorably" on a "substantial" salary increase. Of course, "other factors" must come into play, such as the amount of money allocated to the department for salary increases that year, the personnel department's guideline figures for increases, the amount of the employee's previous increase, and the employee's position on the salary scale for his particular job.

Given the realities of the conventional salary review process, the manager has very little capacity to reward the employee for performance against objectives by using money. Variations from one employee to another are usually so small, within the range of allowable increases, that a pay raise does not usually symbolize performance differences adequately. And in military and civil service organizations, the manager has virtually no influence on the size of pay adjustments, because of the fixed salary scales. Add to this the fact that pay raises come relatively seldom— usually long after some particular accomplishment the employee may take pride in—and we can see how limited the process of "handing out jelly beans" really is.

This means that the manager must have additional forms of reward to offer the employee for high performance. Especially, the employee needs *current rewards*—i.e., fairly immediate and satisfying feedback resulting from his accomplishment. Many of the rewards which satisfy this requirement are psychological rewards. They arise within the employee's transactions with the human environment in which he lives and works. As mentioned in Chapter 5, these take the form of recognition and praise from the manager, recognition from co-workers, and inclusion in the affairs of the work group. But these factors are precisely the ones missing in the Theory-X environment.

Another very painful aspect of the Rat-Race situation stems from the Theory-X manager's attitude toward performance. The confirmed Theory-X manager usually sees human performance as something to be squeezed out of the employee. This attitude contends that, if the employee achieves a certain level of performance, then the clever manager can raise the target level, presumably spurring the employee on to new levels of accomplishment and enhancing the reputation of the manager as one who "gets a lot of work out of people." The employee, however, sees this as a losing game from all angles. So far as the employee sees the situation, "Theory X plus MBO equals Rat Race."

Getting out of the Rat Race requires changing the attitudes of the organization's managers, including the chief executive if necessary. Managers must discover and understand the basic concepts of human behavior in organizations. In particular, they must understand the psychology of punishment and reward if they are ever to mobilize their human resources to high performance. They must create a reward-centered environment, and they must maintain it conscientiously as they direct and guide the work of the employees.

Too Much, Too Soon

Another common pitfall in trying to change an organization with management-by-objectives principles comes from trying to take too big a bite at the beginning. An overly ambitious program can collapse of its own weight and possibly jeopardize long-term acceptance by the members of the organization. The Too-Much, Too-Soon situation typically arises when top management decides to "set up an MBO program," with the expectation of having it fully operational and de-bugged within "three or four months." Experience with formal programs of this type shows that, if they do finally get underway successfully and continue to run well, the process takes about three to five years. The first year of such a formal program usually brings unexpected difficulties, complications, major and minor frustrations, disheartening delays, and even derailments caused by unforeseen problems within the normal work load of the organization.

A situation which might otherwise have resulted in positive attitudes and enthusiastic support from the employees can turn into a state of general confusion when the managers try to do Too Much, Too Soon. But by starting with a small and easily manageable effort, they can whet the appetites of the organization's people for the sense of direction, accomplishment, and personal rewards which they can derive from objectives-oriented working. This new appetite will make the next step easier, and will pave the way for acceptance and support throughout the organization. Chapter 12 gives a general prescription for changing the organization with management-by-objectives principles, within a general framework of "organization development."

The general rule for avoiding the pitfall of Too Much, Too Soon is very simple: Think Big, but Start Small.

11

Practical
Case Histories

Managerial Perceptions

This chapter explores the personal perceptions of practicing managers who have dealt with management by objectives in various forms. The reports I have selected do not, by any means, tell the complete story. They simply provide a multifaceted view which may help to illuminate your thinking about your own approach to the subject. From the many experiences I have had as a consultant and the many discussions I have had with practicing managers, I have selected these few for several specific reasons.

First, these half-dozen cases represent a wide diversity of organizations— large and small, profit-making and nonprofit, product-oriented and services-oriented, and engaged in widely varying kinds of activity. They also show a wide range of managerial opinion about what management by objectives should be and about how well it has worked for them.

Second, they are real. They illustrate actual human experience and tell us what some of our colleagues in the management profession actually think. We need not depend on the hypothetical case and oversimplified situations which so often detract from the credibility of much of the MBO literature.

And third, these reports, brief as they are, give us some insight into the part played by the manager's own *values and biases* in describing a management-by-objectives situation. In almost every major consulting project with which I have been involved, I have noticed vast differences in the perceptions of various people of what the enterprise was all about. Advocates of a new way of doing things tend to see progress and encouraging results simply because they need to and want to. Opponents of a new approach tend to find fault with it at every step and to acknowledge its value only grudgingly.

Managers also vary in the extent to which they, as individuals, approach something new and different with an open, receptive frame of mind. Some people enjoy criticizing any new enterprise, deriving a primitive sense of superiority by showing how smart they are and how dumb the advocates of the new approach are. Such a manager will bring this critical, fault-finding attitude to virtually any new situation.

On the other hand, the manager who makes a personal and political commitment to establishing a new project will probably become biased toward good news, and may even reinterpret the reports of others to meet his own needs for feelings of success. In some cases, this can lead to a highly unrealistic perception of what is happening.

As you read the following accounts, keep in mind that they do not tell you "how well management by objectives works." The answer to that question depends unavoidably on the values and opinions of the person looking at the situation. Remember that they are reports which reflect the *perceptions* of the managers who give them. Following each narrative, I offer a few comments and opinions of my own. Bear in mind that these, too, include my own biases, values, and perspectives. Think all this over and arrive at your own point of view.

Case #1

ORGANIZATION:

A local unit of a well-known international service organization; Executive Director, supported by a paid staff of sixty people and a volunteer board of directors; fifty to one hundred volunteer service workers drawn from the local community

PERSON INTERVIEWED: Executive Director

This executive's remarks: "About two years ago, we received this looseleaf manual here from our headquarters on the East Coast. It contains a complete procedure for making an objectives-oriented plan for our unit's operation. It was written by a consultant who specializes in nonprofit management. They directed us to adopt it as our standard procedure for planning and programming our activities.

"We've used it, and I have no real complaints about it. It works OK. I don't know, . . . I guess I'm more of a 'doer' than a 'planner.' I've been in this business for almost twenty years, and I have a pretty good idea of the needs of our service community, and I've always operated according to clearly stated objectives. So a lot of it is nothing new. I don't believe in making such a formal process out of it.

"I will say, though, that it has forced me to put more things down on paper. Now I make a habit of writing out the year's objectives and spending a few weeks discussing them with our community advisors and board of directors. I think we get better community participation this way. I don't know that the objectives we establish are very much different than those I would develop on my own. But they do get more support from the people involved. I also tend to assign objectives to individual members of my staff more specifically, and to get agreement with them about plans and target dates. I find this helps me to manage better.

"Really, I don't know very much about 'management by objectives.' I just try to have a clear idea of the role this organization ought to play in the community and to set annual goals which help us meet those needs. If that's 'management by objectives,' then I guess I manage by objectives."

COMMENT:

The "East Coast" probably feels a bit lonely, and in need of some assurance that it's really in control. The planning manual is attractive, well-written, and complete. Probably, this executive has improved his methods somewhat and become a little better organized. This organization is very traditional and staid and tends not to requestion its basic purposes. It is presently healthy, and operates on a good economic foundation. If East Coast doesn't push the planning and control function too heavy-handedly, things will probably continue to run pretty smoothly.

Case #2

ORGANIZATION:

A high-technology industrial firm of 2000 employees, engaged in research, design, and production of complex and sophisticated power equipment; company is in a severe business downturn and experiences great uncertainty about its market.

First Person Interviewed: Director of Employee Development and Training

This executive's remarks: "We're trying to implement a very simple program, attempting to get department managers and branch managers across the organization to become more objectives-oriented. In the present confused business situation, and with very few clear corporate goals to start from, they must take the initiative and try to set their own functional goals, no matter how uncertain the process may be. We don't want them to capitulate to despair.

"We're conducting a series of 'refresher' workshops for the managers, focusing on the manager-employee relationship. Most of the employees are highly educated and highly skilled professionals. We're trying to get the managers to do only a few key things.

"First, we want them to discuss their employees' jobs with them and to exchange perceptions of what they should be doing during this period of upheaval.

"Second, we want them to agree on two or three key result areas of the employee's job, and to set a basic objective in each area. And third, we want them to keep in touch with their employees and to follow through on the accomplishment.

"Frankly, we're finding it fairly difficult to accomplish even those limited objectives. Many of our managers are technical experts who have been promoted out of their specialties and into a new kind of situation. They don't have much of a 'feel' for the human side of management. They tend to preoccupy themselves with technical problems, and to ignore their relationships with their employees. This, plus the general condition of low morale, is forcing us to go more slowly than we otherwise might. We've designed a simple one-page worksheet to support the manager-employee dialogue. So far, we don't have a good reading on how well it's working. We're trying to keep the paper work down to an absolute minimum."

Second Person Interviewed: Department Manager in a semiisolated division of the same company

This executive's remarks: "(sigh) I don't know . . . looks like another paper exercise to me. They want us to have a written set of objectives for every single employee and a formal review process. Next, I guess they'll ask for monthly reports and all the rest.

"They put us all through a week of half-day seminars conducted by a management consultant. He did a good job, and he's a very capable guy. But, as far as I'm concerned, we covered a bunch of stuff I already knew. It was a good refresher, but I really didn't learn anything.

"Our operation is a little different from the rest of the company. We make special products, and we have a profitable line. The company's present downturn hasn't affected us as badly as it has lots of other groups. We've always operated on a project-oriented basis, with formal technical and cost objectives, program plans, and all the rest. As far as I'm concerned, we're already managing by objectives. I'm sure we could find some areas where we can improve. But we're operating at a profit, and that's more than most others can say."

COMMENT:

It's sobering to realize how widely two people's perceptions of the same thing can differ. One guy sees a simple change in managerial behavior, where the other sees an impending paper mill. Both of them are intelligent, well-educated, and highly articulate professionals. Without the personal support and direct involvement of one or more top executives, however, the Training Manager is in the classic role of an impotent would-be change agent with very little clout. This forces him to rely on an "epidemiology" model of change—i.e., merely hoping that the benefits of the new approach will sell themselves and that success will be contagious. The simplicity of the approach does favor its long-term success, however. With a long enough attention span and continued patient support, this approach promises to develop more of the organization's managers into objectives-oriented thinkers.

The manager of the profitmaking department admits to using only financial and technical objectives in managing the group. They have set no objectives in any other result areas, such as management development, employee development, organizational climate, or customer relations. Their long-range planning activity is rather modest. Here, we must wonder whether this unit might merely be on the boom side of the classic boom-bust cycle. In this case, the low morale and general level of managerial cynicism will probably work to slow the organization's progress toward the objectives-oriented style of operation. The Training Manager might be well advised to work with a target department whose manager enthusiastically supports the approach and to try to make a notable success story on a pilot basis. This can help to sell the change across the organization. And, the simpler the change, the easier it will be to sell.

Case #3

ORGANIZATION:

A large city government, serving a population of about 1,000,000 people; rapidly growing, diversified community

PERSON INTERVIEWED: Specialist in Organization Development and Training

This executive's remarks: "About five years ago, we got interested in using a program-oriented budget system so we could begin to focus the attention of the various city departments on results and measures of service effectiveness. We figured that, if each department executive and his top management team could develop meaningful measures of the services they provide to the community, then we could allocate costs to those services. Then we'd have a way to establish priorities and balance the budget in terms of maximum service for the taxpayer's dollar.

"It was a neat idea, and I still believe in it. But, I have to say we really haven't done too well. We started with extensive training seminars in management by objectives, and we tried to develop a budget review and analysis process which focused on departmental measures of performance. But it was slow going all the way. I don't think our top executives really understood the thing as well as we thought they did. And the department directors were too busy protecting their own operations and squabbling with one another to really get with it.

"We have a new mayor and a new city manager, as well as changes in the management of several departments. Our brainchild didn't live through the changes very well. Actually, though, as I think back, I have to say that we have made some substantial progress in a number of areas. We still don't have a program budget—we're still struggling with the old activity-centered categorical budget—but many of the departments do plan their operations more along the line of specific objectives for the year. And we've developed much better performance measures in some areas than we had. We've instituted a productivity-improvement project over the last few years that's been getting some impressive results.

"So, all in all, I guess I'd have to say that our reach exceeded our grasp. We were very naive and optimistic about how much we could really accomplish, especially from a staff position without strong top-management direction. Really, I suppose we've done rather well, although we'd like to have done much more."

COMMENT:

This example demonstrates amply the occasional monolithic resistance of a municipal government organization to planned change. It also shows how great can be the difference between a change agent's hopes and expectations and the eventual results. As usual, the change agent's function is organizationally misplaced. Without a position in the management chain, this person will continue to fight an uphill battle. A key city executive, or even an influential department director could lead the way, but most training directors find themselves merely "on call," waiting for somebody else in the organization to mobilize the power and influence to get a program started.

The program-oriented budget offers an excellent means for creating an objectives orientation. The annual budget analysis process provides a natural form for discussing measures of departmental performance and for creating payoff-oriented project areas which city executives can deal with in terms of cost and effectiveness. When the idea finds a top-level sponsor, it will probably take off like a rocket. Until then, it's the same old "ho-hum."

Case #4

ORGANIZATION:

A large Navy center, with several individual commands carrying out diversified fleet-support missions; over 1000 uniformed and civilian personnel

PERSON INTERVIEWED: Former Director of Training, Civilian Personnel Office

This executive's remarks: "I helped set up an MBO program for *X Center* a few years ago. As far as I know, they're still using it. I contacted Dr._____at_____University, and he came out and did a series of seminars to kick off the program. We had an admiral who was really interested in MBO. This guy was a real tiger.

"He got together with all of his captains and set up a formal MBO program for all the commands in the organization. They designed a very formal program, with written objectives, plans, and programs, and a system for monitoring and reporting.

"They had a big meeting in the auditorium; all hands were there. Admiral_____understood the program thoroughly, and he explained to everybody how he wanted it done. It was a highly organized program— very well worked out. And it worked very well. It took a lot of attention and a lot of push from the admiral, but he gave it his personal support.

"But then he left for a new job in Washington, and the next guy who came in really didn't understand it. He kind of thought it was an ongoing system that would be self-perpetuating. Which, of course, it isn't. This guy wouldn't know MBO if it hit him in the head. He was a good administrator, but he really didn't keep the program going. He tended to demand objectives from his subordinates, when they really didn't know what his objectives were.

"I think MBO is really a commonsense approach to good management. I think it really works well if the top guy understands it and gives it his attention. If he doesn't, it just becomes a big mess."

COMMENT:

Here's an interesting example of a situation in which a dedicated and well-informed top executive made an "MBO program" work. He gave it his continuing personal attention and kept it alive by continuously exercising it. It also shows that no formal paper system can sustain itself. It will die without frequent doses of executive support and direct participation. Many Navy organizations—and other military units as well—seem to feed on paper, so in this case a formal system may have seemed quite natural to the people involved. Note also that the system described in this case "belonged" to one executive, who gave it the strength of his authority. A system with no such executive ownership will usually shrivel up and die quickly.

Case #5

ORGANIZATION:

A major hospital, serving a community of about 1,000,000 people; considered by hospital executives to be a well-managed facility

PERSON INTERVIEWED: (Public statement of) Executive Director

This executive's remarks: "Goal setting is a way of life at_____ Hospital. Over the past six years, the hospital's management has continued its vigorous action to raise the quality and value of the organization's goal-setting and objective-setting process."

"Top management launches the yearly goal-setting process approximately four months prior to the beginning of the hospital's next budget period. The hospital's administrative group prepares a 'statement of conditions' that identifies external and internal conditions considered to have significant impact on the goal-setting and objectives-setting efforts of the hospital's managers.

"For the hospital's goal-setting process to be effective at the departmental level, it is essential that objectives be required in every critical area where departmental performance directly affects the achievement of organizational goals. During recent months, the administration has been centering considerable attention on improving four particular aspects of setting departmental objectives. These are: integrating horizontally related objectives, participation of attending medical staff in the hospital's goal/budget system, strengthening the results-oriented features of departmental objectives, and advancing the contributions of staff functions.

"We are currently launching a project to test the feasibility of utilizing managing by objectives as a basis of planning, organizing, and evaluating activities and performance in each of the 'staff' functions of personnel administration, training and education, and management engineering. As a result of achieving more meaningful and measurable outcomes, these staff functions will, in turn, gain greater commitment and support from top administration. We believe it essential to the achievement of an effective system of managing with objectives that the appraisal of management performance be an integral part of the process. We have introduced a new management appraisal process that will evaluate the performance of all managers on the basis of objective setting.

"A weekend retreat was held recently to review last year's goals, to search for reasons why certain goals were not fully attained, and to determine how the goal-setting and objective-setting system could be improved in the months ahead."

COMMENT:

I diagnose this case as an incipient Rat Race, with a strong *Rigor-Mortis* syndrome. The Executive Director of this organization is a dynamic, active individual with a very strong sense of dedication to professional management. But we can read between the lines of the statement and find several indications of anxiety about the whole goal-setting process.

Possibly the executives are beginning to realize how much managerial time and energy goes into the maintenance of the formal system. It has probably survived this long mainly through the efforts of the executive staff, who deal with it every single day. What it does for organizational effectiveness is arguable.

Middle managers and career professionals at this particular hospital often find themselves working long hours on paper work. Many of them feel harrassed, rushed, overworked, and enjoying their jobs less and less. Turnover is increasing, especially among middle managers and technical specialists. The hospital recently experienced an aggressive attempt at unionizing its para-professional workforce. The members of the organization rejected unionization by a narrow margin. Hospital executives have not yet adjusted to this surprising and blunt statement of employee dissatisfaction. I predict this organization will gradually ease off of the intense preoccupation with the Big System and will move toward less formal controls, more employee involvement, and major attempts at improving the organizational climate.

Case #6

ORGANIZATION:

A savings-and-loan association with twenty-three branch offices

This executive's remarks: "We don't use any kind of formal MBO system. In fact, we tend toward less of a formal approach to management than other financial institutions. We believe strongly in the participative management concept, where the individual employee has a lot to say about management decisions and changes that affect his or her job.

"Turnover in our industry is generally high, and it costs us a lot of money to keep hiring and training people. So we try to keep good people with us, mostly by giving them a chance to develop and to play an important part.

"Personally, I tend to use management by objectives as a problem-solving process. I believe in getting to the cause or causes of a problem and setting goals for solving it or making improvements. Then I, as a manager, know what actions to take to get it solved.

"For instance, we recently found that too much of our capital was imprisoned in a nonearning 'liquid' status in the various branch offices. You'd be amazed at how much lost earning power is associated with the everyday working cash that branches handle. So, we studied the problem and found that the tellers were keeping comfortable 'kitties,' to make sure they didn't run out of cash during rush periods and have to go into the back for more.

"The problem was to reduce the amount of drawer cash used but not to make the tellers feel they were being punished. After all, they were trying to do the best job they could. So we worked out a reasonable maximum value for drawer cash and got them to agree to check their levels from time to time. Then they could turn in extra cash and we could get it back into use. Once they understood that the old practice was costing money unnecessarily, they went along with the solution quite quickly. A little bit of training and publicity for the new standard and that was it."

COMMENT:

Enough said.

12

The Organization Development Approach

Thus far, we have reviewed rather critically the major contemporary approaches to management by objectives, as well as the myths and pitfalls to which managers sometimes fall prey. We find much to be wary of in the so-called MBO approach, and we should consider very carefully the sobering lessons learned by those who have had traumatic experiences in trying to make "MBO systems" work.

But we still need a general answer to the questions, "How can managers go about making their organization an objectives-oriented one? How can management by objectives become a constructive, high-performance way of life in an organization?" Everything we have studied thus far points the way clearly to the answer. And that is: *We must start with the organization itself as a human system.* The manager, intervening in the social processes of everyday work life, must act constructively to create and maintain the cybernetic organization described in Chapter 1.

To review briefly: the cybernetic organization has three principal features. They are:

1. *The organization has a reward-centered social climate:* People in the organization receive psychological as well as material rewards for their work; these rewards are plentiful but contingent on successful

job performance; some of them arise from doing the job itself, while others involve formal recognition of the employee's efforts by someone in the organization's power structure; punishment and personal criticism are relatively rare; the emphasis is on recognition of achievement, not on detection of failure.

2. *The organization's managers consistently exhibit an objectives-oriented behavior pattern:* They think and talk in terms of payoffs and achievements; they give job assignments in performance terms; they delegate whole tasks or projects to employees; they grant the maximum autonomy consistent with the individual task, the situation, and the employee; they maintain continual dialogues with their employees concerning payoffs, objectives, and organizational improvements; they reward objectives-oriented behavior on the part of their employees; they praise and reward eagerly, and they punish or scold reluctantly.

3. *The organization's employees consistently exhibit an objectives-oriented behavior pattern:* They discuss job assignments with their bosses in terms of performance and payoffs; they accept higher-level objectives and work out their own implementing objectives and plans; they seek and accept maximum autonomy consistent with the task, the situation, and their own abilities — trying to achieve shared objectives; they take an active interest in the organization's success, and they offer their ideas and suggestions to their bosses for ways to improve it.

The organization becomes a cybernetic entity as it becomes an objectives-oriented organization. For this to come about, virtually everyone in the organization must learn to think and to function "objective-ly" to some extent. This requires a process of total organizational change. The organization's managers, as key action people, have the job of bringing about this organizational metamorphosis constructively and in such a way that the members of the unit find the new way of life more attractive than the old way. They must take the new way self-sustaining. The organization development approach can help to make this happen.

Progress Means Change

An old timer, sitting and rocking on his front porch, remarked to his young visitor, "I've seen a lot of change in my day, young fella. And I've been against all of it."

In trying to build a cybernetic human system, we must first come to terms with a few facts of life concerning change. For no matter how we define it, progress of the kind we want to achieve means change. Certain things which presently go on within the system must diminish or stop altogether. Certain other things which do not presently happen must begin to happen. People must begin to relate to one another in some new ways. The organization's managers and their subordinates must experiment with new patterns of behavior. All this spells *managed change.*

One of the most common expressions in management theory is: "People don't like change." This truism sometimes leads to confusion about change processes within organizations. The statement seems to imply— at least on face value—that people operate like dull, disinterested creatures of habit, seeking routine and repetitive activities and resisting any changes in those activities. Perhaps we should revise this half-true truism to say "People don't like externally imposed changes which do not seem to offer them any better conditions than those they presently know."

In many cases, people do indeed like change. Consider this from your own point of view. If someone offered you a much better job; or a much more attractive (to you) place to live, at the same cost as your present home; or an opportunity for a delightful new experience with no un-desirable features; how would you probably behave? Each of us will eagerly embrace a change, frequently of great magnitude, *if there is something in it for us.* This recalls the WIIFM ("What's In It For Me?") rule of Chapter 3. In order to influence someone's behavior, we must make the new behavior rewarding for that person.

Let's review what we already know about how people—and human systems—respond to external attempts to change their behavior. People will generally adopt new ways of behaving if:

1. They understand the new mode fully and how they as individuals will fit into it.
2. They expect the new mode to bring more benefits or rewards—or at least no fewer—than their present mode.
3. They can see the changes coming, and they have time to adapt to the new mode without unreasonable disruption to their activities.

In terms of practical impacts on their jobs, employees must believe that the managers who propose the changes have considered their interests in the planning process. And we know that getting the employees involved in deciding on the changes and making the plans provides an excellent means for gaining their acceptance and support.

Similarly, we know that people will resist new ways of behaving if:

1. They don't understand the changes and they feel apprehensive about the new mode.
2. They believe the new mode will offer fewer benefits or rewards than the old mode, or they don't know for certain and prefer to stick with what they know.
3. They feel the changes are being forced upon them, with little consideration for their needs or interests.

We need to keep these basic facts firmly in mind as we approach the problem of managing change in any organization.

The Guided Revolution: Managing Change

If we want to bring about constructive changes within the organization which we manage, we had better approach the problem as one of *causing* change rather than forcing change. With this point of view, we can see that useful strategies will have to meet certain specific criteria. First, they must help to facilitate a transition instead of an upheaval. We must bring about the change at a pace which the people can tolerate without undue discomfort. Second, our strategy must help the people of the organization to understand the coming changes. Since they will probably resist adopting a new mode if they cannot understand it, it behooves us to help them in this respect. And third, our strategy must offer recognizable benefits to the people whose behavior we want to change.

We can conceive of the change process in terms of the people as a human system moving from Condition A, characterized by a certain set of behaviors, to Condition B, characterized by new behaviors which we prefer. This point of view amounts to a "guided revolution" approach. Our job as managers and change agents is to facilitate this transition.

We can derive a general framework for changing organizational behavior in terms of specific actions we must take. In general we need to:

1. *Examine the current situation*—Find out for sure what conditions now prevail; evaluate the key human processes in terms of their contribution to organizational health and performance; spot trouble areas and possibilities for improvement.
2. *Specify very clearly the desired new situation*—Identify, as specifically as possible, the new human processes in terms of observable behaviors

and activities; establish realistic objectives for the change process; establish the general time period over which the changes should take place.

3. *Identify management interventions which will facilitate the change* — Explore a wide range of actions, such as training, systems development, planning, establishing special programs, creating special mechanisms for employee action and participation, physical plant changes, etc., and select those which offer the most promise in causing the desired changes.

4. *Make a realistic plan for moving from Condition A to Condition B* — Spell out those management actions you consider necessary and appropriate to bring about the new condition; arrange them according to a realistic timetable, with key milestones and review points along the way; identify key resistance mechanisms and delay factors and find ways to neutralize them; gain the contributions and support of as many people as possible in preparing the plan.

5. *Implement the plan and monitor progress carefully* — Start with areas you can change easily, to create an atmosphere of success and acceptance of change; pay close attention to the reward process, making the new ways of working attractive to the people who must adopt them; stay alert for signs of misunderstanding, frustration, or factionalism which may subvert the transition process; take special actions to neutralize resistance mechanisms or to facilitate areas which need special attention; sell the people on the benefits of Condition B and enlist their active support in bringing it about.

Occasionally, managers and even management consultants will advocate trying to bring about organizational change by a surreptitious, covert process. They seem to proceed from the point of view that the employees would automatically oppose the changes if they knew about them or, that, in any case, they would not want to help with the changes. Here we have another manifestation of the Jackass Myth discussed in Chapter 2. Once the managers of an organization adopt the "us-and-them" point of view in dealing with the employees, they have usually hamstrung their own efforts.

A more enlightened approach calls for ensuring that the change will indeed bring benefits to the members of the organization—or compromising and modifying the proposed Condition B to guarantee that it will—and then publicly sharing the proposed changes with the members of the organization. This means working management-by-objectives methods into the day-to-day processes rather than forcing a new system on them. This will generally lead not only to better understanding and acceptance of subsequent management actions and decisions but also to active support for the changes on the part of those who expect to benefit from them.

Successful change agentry also calls for *realistic expectations* about the time scale of the change process and for patience and persistence in taking the necessary steps according to a realistic timetable. Time and again, action-oriented change agents, such as managers, human resources development people, Affirmative Action officers, industrial engineers, and leaders of employees' groups find themselves surprised and disappointed by the length of time required to bring their pet projects to fruition. History shows that in the typical organization-wide development project—such as Affirmative Action, for example—the first year's effort largely goes into waking people up to the need for change and getting the message to them in competition with all othe other important messages, day-to-day brush fires, and high-priority demands on their time. Some of them will agree with the need and will actively begin to support it. Others will agree but will put it far down the line on their list of things to do. Others will disagree with the need for change and will drag their feet or do nothing to support it. Still others will disagree and will actively oppose the change.

This diversity of response, and particularly the degree of relative indifference to the "hot new idea," may be astounding to the prospective change agent. In place of the enthusiasm and immediate action the change agent may have expected (perhaps unconsciously), there comes a vague "ho-hum" from the organization's general membership. Many change agents find themselves bewildered and even demoralized after a year's time shows much less in the way of tangible results than they expected. Many young and inexperienced employees, long on enthusiasm and short on bitter experience, have found this organizational time lag virtually devastating to their self-images as people of action. This organizational inertia has scuttled many so-called MBO programs simply because the managers who designed them and tried to implement them did not have the long attention spans necessary to get results. Victimized by their own unrealistic expectations, many of them simply lost interest when they did not see the dramatic improvements they hoped for in a short time. A number of experienced management consultants have observed that getting an "MBO program" fully operational and working effectively takes from three to five years. *And at no point does such a system become self-sustaining.* It requires continuous nurturing and renewal by the organization's managers and its people to keep it working.

Management by Objectives
by Objectives

The seemingly repetitive heading of this section is not a misprint nor a type setter's error. It implies that the concept should, if we are to find it useful, apply to itself. That is, we should be able to apply the management-by-objectives concept and its associated problem-solving process to the matter of developing an objectives-oriented organization. This point has a very fundamental significance for the manager who wants to *manage* by objectives, not just to "install a system."

From time to time I have off-handedly asked executives who were in the process of "installing MBO systems" the following question: "What are your objectives in installing this system?" The question usually draws a blank look, a sudden thoughtful expression, and then a variable response. In some cases, the executive answers, "Why, we're going to improve our performance"; or, "To increase the efficiency of the organization"; or, "To make our managers more effective"; or some other equally vague statement. Curiously, the same manager who preaches to the employees about writing specific, measurable goals, with action verbs, deadlines and constraints, cannot state in simple terms what he expects the new system to accomplish for the organization. These executives seem to believe that "MBO" applies to everyone in the organization but them. They have failed to apply the management-by-objectives thinking process to the highest — and most significant — level of intervention in the organization's operation. This kind of intellectual hypocrisy has doomed many an "MBO program" to mediocrity.

In other cases, this probing question triggers a re-examination of the entire enterprise. Often the executives begin to ask, "What *do* we want to accomplish with our organization, and what leads us to believe this system will satisfy our needs when we haven't clearly defined them?" This kind of questioning process leads to some very interesting and enlightening multilogues within the top management circle. It frequently becomes the beginning of a very constructive phase of organization development.

Here's how we use the management-by-objectives approach to the task of building a cybernetic organization. First, let's recall the general management-by-objectives problem-solving process discussed in Chapter 6. The process has five basic steps:

1. State the Problem.
2. Specify the Desired Payoff(s).
3. Spell Out the Desired End Conditions, i.e., Your Objectives.
4. Identify the Possible Actions You Can Take to Meet Them.
5. Make a Plan.

Let's apply the process in a general way, recognizing that the detailed specification of each step will depend on the actual organization, its situation, and the judgements of its managers.

Starting at a general level, we can state the Problem as, "To improve the functioning of the total human system." At this beginning point, we have a fuzzy objective, which we now must convert into specifics which invite management action. We must concede that, at this point at least, we haven't yet done any better than the executive who has decided to "install an MBO system."

But moving to the second step, we can specify the Desired Payoff as, "Making our organization a cybernetic one." Although the terminology of this payoff statement is still somewhat general, note that it quite definitely implies an approach. It focuses on the human factors in organizational performance, for example, as opposed to cost-oriented variables such as productivity and profitability, or functional variables such as production rates and other numerical measures of performance. We have said by this Desired Payoff that we plan an organization-development approach, wherein we will deal with the human system and its human processes.

We can specify the end conditions for the cybernetic organization quite nicely in three Key Result Areas, by referring to Chapter 1. They are:

1. Objectives-oriented managerial behavior
2. Objectives-oriented employee behavior
3. A reward-centered environment

All three of these Key Result Areas offer specific and verifiable end conditions which we can work to bring about and which we can detect once we have achieved them. We can specify and evaluate the goals and subgoals, using the SPIRO criteria (Specific, Payoff-oriented, Intrinsically rewarding, Realistic, and Observable) given in Chapter 6.

The fourth step we will simply describe here in a general way, realizing that the specifics will depend on the particular organization. We can study its current processes and draw upon the judgement and experience of its employees as well as its managers in identifying Possible Actions. This step amounts to identifying the most promising "intervention strategies" which managers can employ to cause the desired changes in the functioning of the organization. And step five, making the Plan, calls for the same straightforward managerial skills one needs in day-to-day supervision. A realistic approach to an organization-development project such as this one might involve a one-year plan for the first "wake-up" phase, during which we create a broad awareness of objectives-oriented thinking and working and begin to develop and reward that kind of behavior on the part of the employees. We introduce certain simple and easily used management tools, but mostly we keep everyone's attention focused on the overall organization development plan. The plan for succeeding years will depend largely on how much we accomplished in the first introductory year.

Let's picture this process of "management by objectives by objectives" as it would actually proceed in a typical medium-sized organization. Let's imagine we have recently taken over the job of chief executive in an organization of about 2000 employees. This might be a manufacturing company, a large government or military agency, a hospital, or a nonprofit public service institution. How shall we apply this thinking process to this organization?

First, we make a careful and thoroughgoing *assessment* of the entire organization. We will probably do well to engage a competent management consultant or other completely neutral person for this step. This will have two advantages. First, it will make a fairly formal process of the assessment. And second, it will eliminate the effects of built-in biases, preconceived solutions, parochial interests, and organizational political relationships. We can make this assessment with certain fairly standard methods, such as a general review of operations, an employee attitude survey, an assessment of the backgrounds and capabilities of all the managers in the organization, and an executive seminar or workshop to explore managerial perceptions of the organization's needs.

We will probably choose to have the results of the assessment phase written up simply and clearly in a report of moderate length. We can then give copies of the report—perhaps in draft form—to the executives and other key action people and ask them to review it and amend its findings as necessary. We will then have a widely accepted statement of our present conditions, problem areas, and opportunities for organizational improvement. To complete the assessment phase, if properly conducted, will probably take about three months.

Next, we will establish objectives for the improvement phase, within the three Key Result Areas of Objectives-Oriented managing, Objectives-Oriented Working, and the Reward-Centered Environment. We might subdivide the first category into areas such as objective-setting skills, problem-solving skills, time-management skills, communication skills, and motivation and reward skills. For each of these subareas, we will identify a set of learnable behaviors, and the associated body of concepts. We can then fix these specific skill-oriented behaviors as *the goals of our organization-development project*. We will require that each of these goals meet the SPIRO criteria mentioned previously.

Similarly, we can subdivide Objectives-Oriented Working into categories like work planning, time management, specific job skills, and communication skills. And we can subdivide the Reward-Centered Environment area into categories like physical surroundings, job design, employee-supervisor relationships, interunit relationships, compensation, career paths and opportunities, opportunities for women and minorities, and employee recreational activities. Others might arise according to the specific nature of the organization. We must take care not to rush this objective-setting phase. This is the critical step in the entire project. We want to keep our expectations realistic and to tackle only that which we feel sure we can handle. At this point, our main interest should lie in assuring a fair degree of success for the program. If we undertake too ambitious a set of objectives for the project, we will eventually find ourselves reviewing our failure rather than taking pride in our success. We should unashamedly stack the cards in our favor by zeroing in on high-payoff areas and moving to provide the most immediate "pain relief" possible.

This judgement process may require an inordinate level of discipline and forbearance on our part, because we may become so excited with the possibilities that we lose sight of the magnitude of the other work we have to do every day. We may underestimate the amount of managerial effort, and even dollar cost required to bring about all these attractive changes. The most important outcome of the first phase of any organization-development project is a feeling of encouragement on the part of those who must carry it out. And this requires, above all, a feeling of success and achievement. So, our sense of the practical tells us: *make the first step a realistic one; rig the game for success.*

Once we have prepared specific written goals for the project, our next logical step is to identify effective *intervention strategies* which will help the people of the organization to accomplish the goals. Certainly, these two steps proceed neither in strict time sequence nor in isolation. For example, selecting a certain goal often implies a definite intervention strategy for achieving it. And, conversely, talking about a well-understood strategy such as training or career development implies certain plausible goals.

Let us recognize also at this point that these goals must become the goals of the members of the organization, not merely the goals of the managers who plan the development project. To the extent that they find the goals reasonable and attractive, the employees can apply their own thoughts and energies to them. In this way, the managers do not find it necessary to manipulate the employees toward the goals. By sharing the goals, the managers and the employees can team up, each contributing their special capabilities and points of view in achieving them.

Intervention strategies are those consciously adopted management actions aimed at achieving the selected goals. The next section discusses a variety of such strategies. Once we have identified the most promising strategies, we can formulate them into a simple and easily followed plan. We will make this a written plan of perhaps ten pages. It will state the overall objectives of the organization-development project and spell out specific goals in each of the three Key Result Areas. It will also prescribe general actions or tasks required and spell out individual responsibilities for the results. Subordinate managers and other key action people will probably want to develop written subplans for their own use as well.

Then we shall begin to do the things called for in the plan and to use our everyday management activities to guide others in their accomplishment of the goals of the project. After six months to a year of patient and persistent effort, we can make a careful review of the organizational situation, and redirect our project as necessary.

Note that this general approach differs markedly from the customary process of "installing an MBO system." It focuses on people, not on paper. And it deals with the human system rather than an abstract paper system. This point of view contends that teaching the members of the organization to behave in objectives-oriented ways is the most effective possible approach to managing by objectives. The real objective of the organization-development project approach is a cybernetic, or objectives-oriented, organization. We achieve that objective by starting with ourselves. We learn to manage by objectives as part of our fundamental approach, and we develop the organization as a natural consequence of that way of managing.

Intervention Strategies

Now let's look at some of the specific management actions we can take in causing desirable changes to happen in the organization. The term "intervention" helps to remind us that our actions in any organization-development project constitute disturbing influences. We bring forces to bear which tend to distort the equilibrium processes and to create new and unfamiliar circumstances to which the people of the organization must adapt. As a general rule, we must make this adaptation process as painless and as attractive as we can, in order for the change to "take" and become permanent.

Training and development programs constitute one of the most useful and most straightforward intervention modes for organization-development projects. Using the various managerial and employee behavior goals as targets, we can design training programs to help people acquire them. *Human relations training* for first-line supervisors frequently offers enormous payoffs in employee morale and commitment to organizational objectives. *Transactional Analysis* has proven to be a very effective system for training supervisors and managers at all levels in basic principles of communicating and motivating.

Other subject areas also offer attractive benefits through the training approach. For example, seminars in managing by objectives, with emphasis on problem solving and objective setting, can help managers acquire the desired new skills. Managers then become teachers for their employees, helping them acquire objectives-oriented working patterns.

One straightforward executive strategy is to buy many copies of a selected book and to issue them to all the managers at a given level of the organization. After giving them time to read and reflect on the book, the executive can bring up the subject for discussion at a staff meeting or a special conference. This offers a very simple and inexpensive way to keep the managers of the organization thinking about good management and renewing themselves and their attitudes.

A variety of other interventions focus on the entire process of *human resources development*, ranging from management development, to team training, to Equal Employment Opportunity programs, to individual training in career development and personal growth. Enlightened organizations are investing in these kinds of programs and are seeing significant payoffs in morale, commitment, and job competence.

An impressive example of the human resources development ("HRD") approach is known as *team building*. This amounts to intensive training of an intact work group, including its leader. Working with a training consultant, the group members examine their own operation, with emphasis on the climate of cooperation and the overall quality of their individual relationships. They study communication and problem-solving techniques applicable to their own daily work and develop a heightened level of awareness of their own interpersonal processes. They learn to establish and maintain a social environment which permits candid discussion of problem areas and which enhances task performance as well as individual motivation and *esprit de corps*. TRW Corporation in Redondo Beach, California, has employed team-building consultants extensively in setting up engineering design groups for high-technology projects. TRW managers report high morale and impressive performance under high-pressure circumstances.

Another common HRD program, Affirmative Action, focuses on the opportunities available to women and minorities. These programs attempt to eliminate or reduce discriminatory treatment in hiring, promotion, placement, compensation, and job opportunity. Sometimes supervisory training and human relations workshops contribute to a better understanding of the problem and open avenues for improvement.

In an organization which suffers from high tension in labor-management relations, the managers may choose to embark upon a project of improving communication between executives and union leaders. This can involve specific programs and joint projects wherein leaders from both "sides" can cooperate in achieving mutual objectives. Workshop sessions, conducted by human relations consultants, can often help these individuals listen to one another more effectively, reduce tension, and find areas of agreement. Organizations such as Kaiser Industries have had success with so-called *labor-management committees,* which work together to improve productivity while maintaining job security and salary benefits for workers. This committee approach had its origins in the early 1920s, with the Baltimore and Ohio Railroad, and has proven itself a number of times. Not all unionized companies, of course, have been so fortunate. But the labor-management committee has frequently served as a constructive alternative to the standard clash between union leaders and company executives. Companies such as Beech Aircraft, Ford Motor Company, General Motors, International Nickel, Rockwell International,

Safeway Stores, and United Parcel Service have well-established labor-management committees.[1]

The avenue of shared payoff for improved productivity, sometimes approached through the *Scanlon plan* or a similar type of program, offers another possibility for developing a healthier organizational climate and promoting employee commitment to company goals. The Scanlon plan, developed by consultant Joseph Scanlon about 1949, involves the use of a base-line productivity figure, computed as the ratio of all direct personnel costs of an operation to the sales value of the production achieved. Employee suggestions which bring productivity improvement result in distribution of the increased profits to the work force. This feedback for objectives-oriented behavior has had some notable success. Plants such as DeSoto, Incorporated, a manufacturer of paints and industrial coatings, have achieved documented increases in productivity.[2] The employees have benefitted directly through increased earnings and indirectly through their sense of accomplishment and participation.

The general term "quality of work life" applies to a variety of developmental approaches to improving the general climate within the organization. The Federal Government created the National Commission on Productivity and Work Quality, in 1970, with two main objectives—"to help increase the productivity of the American economy and to help improve the morale and quality of work of the American worker." This agency became the National Center for Productivity and Quality of Working Life, with the specific mission of creating a public forum for exploring new ways of improving organizational climates while enhancing work productivity.[3]

Quality of Work Life ("QWL") efforts have included Scanlon Plan applications as previously mentioned, joint labor-management committees, and even representation by employees on corporate boards of directors. The latter concept, frequently referred to as *participative management*, has had variable success and acceptance in America. It has frequently found application in a number of European companies.

Another QWL development involves autonomous *employee action*

[1]*Recent Initiatives in Labor-Management Cooperation,* National Center for Productivity and Quality of Working Life, Washington, DC 20036, February, 1976.

[2]*A Plant-Wide Productivity Plan in Action: Three Years of Experience with the Scanlon Plan,* National Center for Productivity and Quality of Working Life, Washington, DC 20036, May, 1975.

[3]*Productivity,* Fourth Annual Report of National Commission on Productivity and Work Quality, Washington, DC 20036, March, 1975.

committees, whose members meet to explore possibilities for improving the environments in their own organizations. J. B. Lansing, Incorporated, manufacturer of high fidelity speaker systems, fostered the birth and growth of an employee group which made a series of highly constructive recommendations to top management. In the great majority of cases, the company's management enthusiastically adopted the committee's proposals.

QWL improvements extend to many aspects of the social system within the organization. *Flexible working hours,* for example, offer employees greater autonomy and self-determination in getting their work done. "Flextime" also offers advantages to working mothers who must arrange for child care or adapt to public school schedules. Occidential Life Insurance has experimented extensively with flextime arrangements, with generally pleasing results. Occidental's management found that absenteeism dropped, as employees could use their own time more effectively for personal business. Productivity also held steady, despite the apprehension of some executives about the lack of 100 percent overlap between workers whose jobs required cooperative activity. Some companies have also discovered the value of increased use of part-time employees, working variable schedules which meet their own needs and provide flexibility in manpower allocation.

Other QWL interventions designed to create a reward-centered environment involve changes to the work processes themselves. One such approach focuses on autonomous work groups, in which the employees team up to produce a completed product or to carry out a complete process. Their managers often delegate a great deal of latitude to them in laying out their work activities, scheduling various tasks, deciding how best to sequence the operations, and even making improvements in their production processes.

A widely reported example of this mode of organization development is the Rushton Mining Company in Pennsylvania. There, company management induced a shift in the conventional foreman-worker relationship, reducing some of the autocratic power of foremen and increasing their responsibilities in the areas of training, safety, and methods improvement. Rushton people experienced fairly dramatic reductions in accident rates, safety violations, supply costs, and other morale-related problem areas.

The technique of *job sharing* provides another flexible alternative to standard patterns of work. In this mode, two or even more employees work on a less-than-full-time schedule, sharing the same individual job.

Each works a portion of a regular shift, depending on his or her needs and desires. This approach brings higher administrative costs and requires more attention from supervisors, but it offers distinct advantages in morale and commitment from employees who focus their attention on completed projects rather than on continuing day-to-day "working."

Job enrichment has also shown dramatic results in a number of cases. In this mode of organization development, the supervisor and the employee jointly redesign the employee's job, adding tasks and experiences which make the job more challenging and rewarding while improving productivity in the broader organizational sense. This represents a divergence from Frederick Taylor's post-Industrial Revolution theory of reducing the job to its simplest mechanistic form. Many organizations have deliberately complicated certain jobs, thereby making them less boring and monotonous, and incidentally capitalizing on previously unused employee skills.

Cutler-Hammer's management reorganized the work stations at a Milwaukee plant, eliminating or combining monotonous converyor-belt operations and permitting an adaptive team approach to the assembly of electrical equipment. Employees could then move about within the operations area, interacting with one another more frequently and teaming up on bottleneck tasks to keep the production level up. The enriched-task activities brought increased productivity, lower absenteeism and turnover, and consistently high morale.

Environmental engineering offers yet another creative intervention in the organization's operations. This involves rearranging or redesigning the physical setting in which people do their work. By considering the psychological features of spatial arrangement; human contact patterns; effects of light, form, and color; safety features; noise levels; and various aspects of privacy and human "territory," the designer of a building or facility can make a very large impact on the general morale and psychological processes of the people who work there.

New fields such as architectural psychology have come into their own through applications such as these. Executives of one large marketing organization found that absenteeism increased and productivity dropped sharply after they moved the organization into a fancy new suite of offices. Employee morale declined as well. A review of the facility shows that the color schemes, relative arrangement of work stations, and human contact patterns tended to depress the people working there. This led to redesign and redecorating schemes for improving the quality of the physical surroundings.

All of these options should be considered merely that—options. In bringing about the three key kinds of conditions—i.e., objectives-oriented managing, objectives-oriented working, and a reward-centered environment—we must use our best judgement and select those options which seem right for the particular organization, its people, and its processes at a particular time. Infatuation with "the latest thing" can bring disaster just as swiftly as regression to the inhuman, Theory-X patterns of the past. The greatest danger inherent in experimenting with QWL programs is in being victimized by fads. And the greatest potential is in releasing human capability and fostering that precious condition of employee involvement and commitment to the health of the organization. As Peter Drucker has observed, "The job of management is to liberate, rather than contain the worker."

Effective Managerial Behaviors

Virtually every organization-development program can benefit from emphasis on one key element of the psychological climate, namely the effects of managerial behavior on employee morale. Many psychological studies and years of commonsense experience have shown the clear-cut cause-and-effect relationship between how the organization's appointed leaders treat their subordinates and the attitudes the subordinates have about working there. Executives of the State of California's Department of Motor Vehicles, for example, decided to have the organization's employees evaluate their supervisors. Using an anonymous survey procedure, they developed effectiveness profiles for every supervisor and manager in the organization and fed these results back to them. The results caused consternation for some managers and satisfaction for others. In this unprecedented move, the executives of the organization put all its managers on notice that they would be held accountable for employee attitudes which stemmed from manager-employee relationships. The names of people who have quit organizations or transferred out of high-paying and challenging jobs because they would not tolerate degrading and inconsiderate treatment from their bosses would fill a large book. The prevalence of inconsiderate treatment, especially by first-line supervisors, testifies to the high pressure of the management job and to the difficulty most ordinary people have in coping with it when they get promoted into the supervisory ranks.

We could attribute most of the toxic environmental factors in a typical organization to the failure of top managers to recognize the need for human relations skills and an understanding of basic psychology on the part of their subordinate managers.

We could devote an entire book to the topic of communication and human relations for managers, of course, but let us at least summarize here some of the key behaviors which managers at all levels can recognize and consciously develop. These specific skills can form the basis for effective training seminars for managers at all levels, designed to promote behavior which improves the organizational climate:

1. *Process observation*—Tuning in to the human and personal side of business transactions routinely and attentively; observing behavior patterns which people bring to various situations; spotting role-oriented behavior and detecting the apparent roles which individuals seem to adopt toward one another; routinely observing relationships between pairs of people and among members of small groups; observing and assessing the manager's own relationships with various people in the organization; spotting deadlocks; adversary situations, misunderstandings; and counterproductive competition among managers as well as employees; observing helpful and counterproductive dynamics within small task groups.

2. *Listening*—Staying alert for new information and ideas; listening attentively to what employees as well as other managers have to say; showing respect for the capabilities and contributions of others by soliciting their ideas; listening actively; using techniques such as questioning, paraphrasing, feedback, and maintaining empathy.

3. *Communication maintenance*—Paying special attention to helping others get their ideas across; encouraging employees to express ideas and opinions; using statements which clarify, maintain empathy, encourage others to communicate, and avoid misunderstanding; maintaining an open climate within the work group, in which employees can voice opinions without fear of intimidation or disapproval; teaching effective communication techniques to employees; praising effective communication behavior.

4. *"Stroking"*—Giving unconditional "strokes," i.e., acceptance and recognition messages directed to the employee as an individual; simple but important acts such as saying "hello" every morning, stopping to chat briefly about topics of interest to the employee; showing interest in the employee as a person.[4]

5. *Affirmation*—saying things to the employee—and backing them up with action—which shows that the manager accepts the employee as

[4]For a practical view of supportive human transactions, see Jut Meininger, *Success Through Transactional Analysis* (New York: Signet, 1973).

a person and *expects the employee to do well;* giving praise and public recognition for a well-done task; watching for "praiseable" behavior; selecting specific target behaviors for enhancement or reinforcement and systematically rewarding them; generally ignoring or otherwise not rewarding undesirable behavior; *not* giving praise and compliments too cheaply or so profusely as to weaken their effect.

We can consider all of these managerial behaviors to constitute a reward-centered pattern of dealing with employees. If consistently applied, they will create and maintain the reward-centered environment so essential for management by objectives. Note that these management actions focus on the employee as an individual human being, and they service that person's needs for feelings of acceptance, personal importance, and achievement. Some managers have developed this rewarding style of interpersonal relations so well that employees and managerial colleagues find them personally attractive and enjoyable to be with. Others have evolved such an abrasive personal style that their subordinates and colleagues tend to avoid them as much as possible.

We can differentiate these two extremes of managerial behavior as a "punishing" interpersonal style and a "rewarding" style. To determine whether a particular managerial behavior is punishing or rewarding, we have only to check the reaction of the "recipient." An employee, or any other working associate of the manager, will not usually come back for more of those experiences he finds personally unpleasant. This constitutes the basic definition of a punishing transaction. Similarly, a rewarding transaction is one which the other person would feel good about repeating. Many "tough-guy" managers unthinkingly "punish" others in their day-to-day transactions. That is, the other person experiences the transaction as a matter of getting punished for doing whatever he or she has just done. For example, the manager who criticizes or tears apart the report an employee has just brought in for review has actually punished the employee for coming into the office. The manager who makes a habit of this kind of transacting may wonder why he or she finds it so difficult to get staff members to come into the office and report the status of their projects. Similarly, the manager who blasts an employee with scolding, personal abuse and accusations when the employee brings in a problem or confesses to having made a blunder has punished that person for being honest and seeking to rectify the situation. Such a manager should not wonder that the employees cover up problems and put off coming in for assistance. The manager has trained them to do just that.

Conversely, the manager with a rewarding interpersonal style generally leaves the employee with a feeling of accomplishment and affirmation, even in problem situations. This manager takes a few moments in reviewing the report to notice the quality of the job and praise the employee honestly and emphatically for it. This recognition must not serve as a prelude to the "bad news" or as a mumbled ritual. In most cases, the employee will consider the job well-done—if the manager has set a high standard for performance—and will expect some recognition of that fact. Simply taking the time to give that needed praise constitutes a rewarding behavior on the manager's part.

This notion of punishing and rewarding transactions extends to the smallest aspects of the manager's behavior. The punishing manager scolds, criticizes, ridicules, overlooks good performance, concentrates on mistakes and shortcomings, withholds expected strokes or praise, ignores employees except for selfish purposes, accuses, threatens, cuts off honest dissent, suppresses employee opinions, rejects feedback, demands unreasonable performance, intimidates others, and makes them feel defensive.

The rewarding manager strokes others unconditionally, listens attentively, gives praise for a job well done, accepts others as human and capable of making mistakes, sets a high standard for employees and rewards them for achieving it, challenges their thinking, invites and accepts feedback, encourages constructive controversy and dissent, makes reasonable assignments, focuses conversation on achievements and new goals, puts others at ease, shows respect for their ideas, focuses on problems instead of personal shortcomings, and nutures high-quality relationships with working associates.

This inventory of managerial behaviors underscores the fundamental importance of the boss-employee relationship. In virtually any organization, top management can profitably begin with human relations development programs to teach rewarding behavior patterns to the managers and other action people. And the inner circle of top-management people is the best place to start. As the members of the executive team adopt rewarding styles of dealing with each other, they will quite naturally extend these patterns to dealing with their subordinate managers. Those managers will, in turn, find it easier to deal with their employees in the same way. With the sincere support and participation of the chief executive and the top-level team, training programs in human relations can bring remarkable results in improving the organizational climate.

13

Review and Reminders

This chapter sums up and reviews some of the key concepts of the book. After reading the book, you may find this chapter helpful as a ready reference source for some of the main ideas of interest to you. If you've just discovered the book and are browsing through this chapter in hopes of merely picking up the major ideas, remember that the meaning which the following review material has for you will depend on the extent to which you've thought about the underlying concepts. If you simply want to "read and run," do so with my blessing. But please don't overestimate how much you know about the ideas in *this book* from such a brief exposure.

Many of these ideas run counter to popular "MBO" practice, and you should be fully aware of the effects of these differences. I make a special plea here that you do not try to use this book—or any other, for that matter—as a "cookbook" for management by objectives. Use it as a way to add perspective to your thinking and possibly as a way to avoid some of the more punishing pitfalls. With that caution, let's proceed with the review.

The Three Basic Conditions for Management by Objectives

1. Objectives-oriented managers
2. Objectives-oriented workers
3. A reward-centered environment

Ten Commandments of Management by Objectives

1. Start with *Yourself* and Your Own Work Habits.
2. Avoid the *Paper Trap.*
3. *Teach* Your Subordinates to Think Payoff.
4. Create a *Reward-Centered Environment.*
5. Be Demanding; Expect *Results,* Not Just Action.
6. Be *Human* and Allow Others to Be Human.
7. Have a Clear Idea of Your Organization's *"Next Move."*
8. *Concentrate* Your Resources on a Few Key Result Areas.
9. Have *Realistic Expectations* about Planned Change.
10. Spend Your Day Getting the Really *Important Things Done;* Don't Worry about the Small Stuff.

Management Myths

Many managers have fallen victim to these misconceptions about organizations, people, and the job of managing. Keep alert for them, and make sure they don't creep into your thinking processes. Refer to Chapter 2 for detailed discussions.

1. The Cookbook Myth
2. The Machinery Myth
3. The Robot Myth
4. The Jackass Myth
5. The Accountability Myth
6. The Visibility Myth

Most Common "MBO" Pitfalls

Here are some of the most frequent pitfalls managers find themselves in, especially those who attempt to implement overambitious "MBO systems." See Chapter 10 for detailed discussion.

1. The *Rigor-Mortis* Trap
2. The Paper Jungle
3. Objectives for the Sake of Objectives
4. The Self-Made Prison
5. The Rat-Race Trap
6. Too Much, Too Soon

How to Recognize the Activity Trap

The following symptoms provide clues to Activity-Trap situations. Not every Activity Trap will have all of these features, but a preponderance of them usually gives good evidence that Parkinson's Law is working.

1. The manager is usually overworked, harried, and unable to make time for planning and creative thinking.
2. People may be busy, but most of them can't explain their parts in the "big picture."
3. Few, if any, of the people can explain the organization's goals or overall strategy in simple terms.
4. The organization's manager can't describe the big picture in simple and convincing terms.
5. Many people preoccupy themselves with methods, procedures, and paper work, to which they refer euphemistically as "management tools."
6. The manager places great emphasis on employees arriving for work on time, keeping regular lunch and break schedules, and "keeping busy."
7. There may be a widespread attitude of "Don't ask me—I only work here."
8. A frequently heard statement is "That's not my job."
9. Factionalism, in-fighting, and personal politics are on the increase.
10. People express feelings of frustration, lack of interest, and resentment toward their work.

Suggestions for
Top Managers

1. Develop an objectives-oriented organization, starting with *yourself* and the top-management team.
2. *Avoid* the quagmire of the organization-wide paper "MBO system."
3. Question the basic *values and directions* of the enterprise from time to time.
4. Develop a meaningful definition of *"Our Business,"* regardless of the effort, agony, and time it may take.
5. Get out of your fancy office from time to time and *get in touch* with the people of your organization; find out what they're thinking.
6. Accept responsibility for the overall organizational climate *you have created;* deal with it as you would any other aspect of executive management.
7. *Model* those behaviors yourself which you want your subordinate managers to adopt.
8. *Reward* subordinate managers for objectives-oriented thinking and managing.
9. Don't try to manage everybody in the organization; *manage those managers* within your own sphere of direct influence.
10. Work smart—not hard; protect your own health, well-being, and creative energies as *critical organizational resources.*

Suggestions for
Operational Managers

1. Assess your own *managerial style* and its impact on your unit's operation.
2. Develop a *rewarding* interpersonal style of dealing with employees and colleagues.
3. *Teach* your employees the objectives-oriented pattern of working.
4. Develop a *master plan* for your group's operation.
5. Keep your management methods, systems, procedures, and plans as *simple* as practically possible.
6. Develop an *assertive attitude* toward demands on your time.
7. Allocate your efforts each day according to a system of *priorities.*
8. Use objectives to shape your *decisions.*

9. Use objectives to *elicit performance* from your employees, not as a means to evaluate them as people.

10. Work smart—not hard; *go after results,* and avoid the managerial treadmill of long hours and unproductive activity.

Analyzing Your Own Managerial Style

1. To what extent to you grant *autonomy* to your employees?

2. To what extent to you define their jobs and responsibilities in *performance* terms?

3. To what extent do you assign tasks which provide opportunities for *"closure"* experiences?

4. How often do you give *praise or compliments* for a job well done?

5. How often do you make the "howdy rounds," making *contact* with your employees and giving unconditional "strokes"?

6. To what extent do you put an employee *at ease* and make communication easy in one-to-one situations?

7. How well do you show your employees that you are *approachable* and that you value their ideas and opinions?

8. To what extent do you promote *team behavior* and reward cooperative working?

9. What kind of a *working atmosphere* have you created in your unit?

10. How do your employees seem to feel *about you* as a manager and about their relationships with you?

Developing Objectives- oriented Employees

1. Demonstrate objectives-oriented behavior on your own part whenever possible, to let your employees know you practice what you preach.

2. Use performance-oriented terms regularly in your conversation. Discuss values, payoffs, objectives, performance levels, and measures of accomplishment.

3. Begin to specify assignments in performance terms. Spell out the big picture and the desired payoff. Make clear to the employee what you consider a properly completed job. Strive to make this an everyday habit.

4. Assess your own management style, with emphasis on your willingness to grant autonomy—to let go of important tasks and give them over to your employees for completion. Identify opportunities to lighten your work load by delegating complete tasks or problems.

5. Assess the employee and the job in combination. What is the nature of the work? How much of it can or should you delegate completely to the employee's control? What opportunities exist for closure experiences? To what extent has the employee demonstrated that he can or wants to accept greater job autonomy?

6. Encourage each employee to plan out those aspects of his job which are not matters of routine. Require that each worker who is engaged in an assigned project be able to explain in simple terms how he plans to accomplish the task and what measures of achievement he will use in assessing his work.

7. Hold a review conference with each of your employees, and plan to repeat it every three to six months. Discuss the various performance aspects of the job, and give the employee a chance to clarify his thinking. Invite him to think of the job in terms of accomplishment rather than merely activity. Solicit the employee's ideas on ways to increase the contribution he can make to the organization by means of his job and his activities.

8. Hold occasional unit meetings to let your employees know how they are doing as a team and to share your views of the future. Encourage evaluations by group members, and solicit their contributions to your decisions about future directions.

9. Reward accomplishment, not merely activity. Give compliments for a job well done. Be free with praise and honest compliments. Don't overdo it, but don't underdo it either.

10. Be demanding. Make performance an organizational ethic. Talk about it, specify it, require it, and reward it. Try in every way possible to reward employees for independent problem solving and acceptance of responsibility. By actions and interactions, create and maintain an atmosphere which permits honest mistakes. Be quick to reward and slow to punish.

Suggestions for the Objectives-oriented Employee

Your career success depends largely on your ability to accomplish worthwhile results and to prove to your boss that you can take an objectives-oriented approach to your job. Here are some important tips:

1. Think about your job in terms of *accomplishment;* focus on the payoffs of your activities.

2. Try to see the work of the unit from the *boss's point of view;* make his or her problems your own problems and help whenever possible to solve them.

3. Demonstrate to the boss that you can *work on your own*, without a lot of supervisory hand holding.

4. Look around for *performance opportunities* the boss might not have recognized; find ways to do your job better.

5. Sell your ideas to the boss in terms of *payoffs*; focus on worthwhile objectives, or show how your proposal will help to achieve accepted objectives.

6. Keep in touch with the boss; keep him or her *informed* about your work, and *anticipate* upcoming problems.

7. Don't become totally enslaved to the organization just to keep your job; maintain a healthy sense of *your own worth* as an individual, and have a clear idea of your career objectives and personal values.

8. Expect to be treated as a human being; insist that *your needs* for involvement and a sense of accomplishment be recognized and accounted for.

9. Manage your own time as effectively as you can; get the *really important jobs* done first.

10. Don't assume the boss has a cast-iron ego; *say so* from time to time when you think he or she is doing a good job.

The Management by Objectives Problem-solving Process

To make your thinking processes and your decisions more goal-oriented, develop the habit of approaching action situations with this problem-solving model:

1. State the problem.
2. Decide what payoff you want from the situation. }   I. "Fuzzy" phase

3. Specify goals which will assure the payoff. }   II. Goal-setting phase

4. Identify actions which will achieve these goals.
5. Make a plan for achieving the goals. }   III. Action phase

Selecting an Organizational Strategy

Setting the organization's strategy, i.e., its "next move" in the marketplace it serves, involves five basic steps:

1. Evaluate the current state of the organization's *"environmental match."*
2. Study the environment and identify important *changes* and trends which will affect the organization.
3. Specify the nature of the environmental match you want to establish and how to achieve it, i.e., your organization's "next move."
4. Set *goals* which spell out the desired end conditions for a selected point in time.
5. Decide what *actions* and organizational changes are necessary to achieve the goals, and make a strategic plan for achieving them.

Analyzing Your Organization's Environment

Consider at least the following subenvironments in assessing your organization's environmental match:

1. Customer Environment
2. Competitive Environment
3. Economic Environment
4. Social Environment
5. Technological Environment
6. Political Environment
7. Legal Environment
8. Physical Environment

Strategic Planning

1. Get the entire top-management *team* involved in the process.
2. Allow plenty of freedom for *constructive controversy*, creative thinking, and useful debate; use seminar-style executive sessions.
3. Question the organization's basic philosophies from time to time; make planning a *continuous* process, not an annual event.
4. *Support* the thinking and planning process with comprehensive studies, planning data, and management analyses where needed.
5. *Don't delegate* the planning process to a "planner"; have one executive put together the plan, but only after all members of the team have contributed their ideas and opinions.
6. Have a *written plan* which is simple, fairly brief, and specific; make it available throughout the organization to those who need to understand it and work to meet its goals.

7. *Focus* the plan on just a few Key Result Areas of high payoff; don't dissipate energy and resources with a multitude of objectives which obscure the real winners.

8. Gain *commitment* for the plan throughout the organization by including the key action people in the planning process to whatever extent is feasible.

9. Make the plan *reasonable;* focus on realistic achievement.

10. Build into the plan an automatic process for *reviewing* it from time to time, for *changing* it as necessary, and even for *abandoning* major portions of it if unforeseen circumstances require it.

Index